University Interviews Guide

Second Edition

Andy Gardner
and
Barbara Hamnett

Copies of this publication may be obtained by contacting:
Prospects sales and marketing:
Tel: 01229 814840
Email: info@prospects-sales.co.uk
www.prospects-sales.co.uk

Published by
JFS School
The Mall, Kenton
Harrow HA3 9TE

Editor: Sarah Cunningham
Cover designer: Sarah Pearson

This publication has been partly funded by the Raising Achievement Partnership
Programme, Specialist Schools and Academies Trust.
The named authors alone are responsible for the views expressed in this publication.

British Library Cataloguing-in-Publication Data
A catalogue record for this book is available from the British Library.

ISBN 978-0-9548245-1-8

Printed in England by Fingerprints, Barrow.

Contents

Foreword

In the JFS sixth form it is standard policy for every student to experience a preparatory interview with a senior member of staff before their UCAS Apply is completed. The aim is to help students secure places on their chosen courses, to ensure that their personal statements are a reflection of their choice of course and to prepare them for university interviews generally. The interviewer will not normally know the student well and may be able to offer new reflections not only on the UCAS Apply itself, but on commitment, personal qualities and general guidance.

For more than thirty years we have been asking sixth-formers to complete feedback forms when they have returned from interviews at universities. These provide a rich resource, an essential companion, for subsequent students to tap into for help with both personal statements and interviews. The collection of feedback forms has provided the basis for this book and we are very grateful to the generations of JFS students whose contributions have made this publication possible. We are also extremely grateful to students at La Swap Sixth Form Consortium for their generous donation of questions.

Barbara Hamnett
Former principal deputy headteacher, JFS School

Acknowledgements

Our thanks are due to every JFS and La Swap sixth-former who filled out a feedback form or sent us an email and thereby contributed to the source material for this book. It would not have been possible without them. Many thanks also to: Alexandra Galvin from SSAT RAPP, Pamela Toussaint of Southampton Solent University, Helen Furman; Pat Maxted, Tim Miller, Patricia Kirby, Mary Nithiy, Alex Dawes, Graham Sargen, Nick Calogirou and Pete Williamson from JFS; Emma Jones and Brian McGowan from La Swap; Peter Bournsell from Brent AimHigher; Nigel Bowles of St Anne's College, Oxford; Mike Sewell of Selwyn College, Cambridge; Richard Partington of Churchill College, Cambridge; Stephen Grundy, Community Team, SSAT; Harriet Nerva.

Introduction: Why and how to use this guide

You may be asking yourself, 'What is the point of this book?' The commonly held belief, it seems, is that universities do not interview applicants any more. We would like to disagree with this view. While we accept that interviews are a very labour-intensive method of selection, and we can see that universities may be looking at ways to reduce the number of applicants that they interview, interviews are still happening in large numbers and applicants should be prepared for them. In fact, in the case of degree courses that train for a specific career, applicants are still highly likely to be interviewed. And some universities still interview *all* applicants who make it past the initial selection process.

In any case, even if your university application results in no interviews at all, preparing yourself as if for an interview can be extremely helpful and will be useful in preparing your personal statement. Looking at the sample interview questions in this guide, both general and subject-specific, will improve your self-awareness and give you much more of an idea about whether the course you have chosen is really the one for you.

The guide is split into two parts. Part One covers the general aspects of preparing for interviews and is broken into six sections as follows:

- **'Why have you applied for this course?'** This is the question you are most likely to be asked in any interview. But would you know how to answer it in a logical way? We believe that to know where you are going you need to know where you have been! This section of the book will help you retrace your steps through the thought processes that led to your choice. Once you are clear about how you came to your decision, you should be able to answer this question.
- **'Tell me more about yourself'** This section contains a list of questions you could be asked in an interview, whatever subject you apply for. They have *not* been made up! In fact, they are all questions that have been asked in interviews attended by students from the JFS and La Swap Sixth Form Centres in London in recent years. Do, also, look at the students' comments about their interview experiences: they are often enlightening.
- **'Is there anything you'd like to ask?'** You will find here some general tips about how to deal with this question, but the most important thing is to make sure you ask a question that you really do want to ask, rather than just going through the motions.
- **Personal preparation and presentation** This section offers very general advice about what to expect, how to prepare yourself and how to make a good impression. If you are applying after a gap year, make sure that you have re-captured some of your academic work such as texts studied for A Level. It is easy to forget.

New to the second edition:

- **Applying for medicine** This section has been written by someone who has recently and successfully been through the process of applying to study medicine and who is able to offer invaluable insights into the process.
- **A realistic application for Oxbridge** This is aimed at teachers and higher education advisers who want to give their brightest students a chance to shine in interviews for Oxford and Cambridge using the newly developed GRIST framework.

Part Two of the guide is an A-Z of university subjects, with information and advice about what to expect in an interview for each subject. Remember that interviewers will be trying to discover:

- how much you already know about the subject you have chosen;
- whether you have the aptitude and thinking skills to learn more;
- whether you have thought about what the degree course will involve.

Information under each subject covers the following areas.

- **Essential/useful A levels** (including AGCEs and Diplomas) We still come across sixth-formers with misconceptions about what qualifications they need to do certain courses.
- **Your chance of being interviewed** No authoritative surveys have been carried out on this. The opinions here are those of the authors.
- **What you need to know** Some essential pointers – ignore them at your peril!
- **Sample interview questions and students' comments** Again, these are drawn from the interview experiences, largely, of JFS and La Swap sixth-formers.

We accept that we have not been able to include every one of the many degree courses available. We hope you will look at the entries for related subjects in order to get an idea of what an interview in your own subject may be like.

Finally, please note that we have given you the questions here, but we have most definitely not tried to give you the answers. This is deliberate! The answers are for *you* to decide.

Printed in England by Fingerprints, Barrow-in-Furness.

Part One: General aspects

1. 'Why have you applied for this course?'

The question that crops up in interviews time after time is simply this: 'Why have you applied for *this* course at *this* university?' It is therefore essential to have your reasons clear in your mind (an answer such as 'I think it will be interesting, fun, exciting, etc.' is really not adequate). If you are completely sure about your reasons for applying, you will be much better equipped to respond confidently to an interviewer, who will be looking to discover your motivations and commitment to the course.

The best way to clarify your ideas is to go back over the thought processes that led to your decision in the first place. So, think back.

Choosing your subject

Initially, you probably asked yourself the following questions.

- 'Am I interested in continuing to study something that I enjoyed at A level/AGCE (Applied GCE – double award A Level)/Diploma?'
- 'Do I want to do something that leads to a certain career?'
- 'Do I want to study something new that I feel I might be very interested in?'

Look at the following two examples. Do either of them reflect your own decision-making? The first is simple and straightforward. The second is more complex, and probably closer to reality.

Example 1
'I'm enjoying and doing very well in my maths A level. I don't have a definite career idea yet and I'm not interested in studying anything new. I have looked at related degrees such as economics, computing and management studies but I feel that I would like to take the maths to a higher level at university.'

Example 2
'I am doing politics A level along with English and history. My strengths are very much in the essay-based subjects. I am thinking about studying politics with philosophy and I may want to become a solicitor.'

The second example encompasses all three of your initial questions: you would be carrying on with politics; you would be able to enter your chosen career after doing a CPE (Common Professional Examination) conversion course; and you are picking up a new subject that you think will interest you. It is probable that you had originally considered doing a law degree but you realized that, for law, the actual university you go to is very important and you felt it would be easier to get on to a politics and philosophy course than a law course.

Now let us look at each of the initial questions in turn and consider some of the additional factors that should have influenced your decision.

If you have chosen a subject based on your A level/AGCE/Diploma subjects, did you consider the following?
- Even if you do a degree that is a continuation of one of your A levels, there are still going to be marked differences in content. For example: an economics degree will involve far more statistics than the A level; a biology degree will include far more chemistry than the A level (hence the common requirement for chemistry A level).
- Some arts subjects, such as English, are incredibly competitive – the standard offer from most traditional universities would be AAB or higher. Did you consider whether you could get what you wanted from a degree by studying some other subject (for example, modern languages, philosophy, cultural studies, American studies, modern European studies)?
- Science degrees in subjects related to A levels (chemistry, physics, biology, maths) are much more flexible in their entry requirements, especially at the clearing stage. The difference in the range of choices open to a student with three arts A levels at CCC and a student with three science A levels at CCC are striking.
- Even if you do not know what career you would like to go into, and you have therefore chosen a subject you have enjoyed at A level, did you still think about the career implications?

If you have chosen a subject based on your ideas about your future career, did you consider the following?
- A large number of careers now have graduate-only entry – either officially or unofficially. Teaching, professional surveying, professional engineering, chartered accountancy and medicine are some examples.
- Some careers require a specific degree (for example, pharmacy, hotel management) while others just require a degree (for example, chartered accountancy, retail management). It is worth noting that for some careers, such as chartered accountancy, employers can be very concerned about your original A level results.
- If you choose a degree that is career specific then it must match your own personal profile. Does it reflect your interests, does it suit your abilities, does it accord with your values and attitudes? The way to find out is to do some research: if possible get some work experience; talk to people who work in the career area; look at information in careers libraries and on the internet.
- What if you change your mind? How easy will it be to gain entry to another career field? This will vary from one vocational degree to another, but very often core skills gained in one degree can be useful for another career area. For example, a primary teaching graduate will have acquired very useful communication skills that can be applied to other areas of work.

If you have chosen a subject based on developing an interest in something new, did you consider the following?
- New subjects can be divided into two categories: degrees with a career link and degrees with no obvious career link. Which is yours?
- Examples of degrees *without* an obvious career link include anthropology, philosophy and classics. Students choosing such subjects are prompted by their personal interests, but they also need to read up about their subject and research courses through university prospectuses. People, particularly parents, often worry about the employment prospects of these graduates; in fact, their levels of employment tend to be the same as for other non-vocational graduates.
- Examples of degrees *with* a career link include psychology (though only a minority of these graduates become professional psychologists) and media studies (though such graduates are in no way guaranteed entry into the media). Remember that the main reason to study these subjects is that you are very interested in the content of the course – what may follow on from them in terms of a career is a bonus!

Choosing a university

Let us now presume that your decision about what to study has been made. How did you then narrow down your choices to the five you put in UCAS Apply? Your main considerations would probably have been: course content; your predicted grades; the location of the university; the reputation of the university.

Course content
- Many degrees will be very similar to each other, either because they have to meet the requirements of professional bodies (for example, law, medicine, psychology, electrical engineering) or because past practice has led to degrees in certain fields having similar content (business studies is one of these).
- If course content was fairly similar, did you look into the methods of assessment (exams, assessments, modules) as a means of narrowing down your choices? Different methods of assessment suit different people.
- On the other hand, some degrees with the same title vary greatly in content (geography, history, media studies and languages are examples). Did you look closely at the course information to see what you would be getting?
- Some courses provide great variety through the range of options on offer. Some universities have an in-built system for giving you a wide range of choice (for example, through faculties). Did this influence your decision?

Predicted grades
- These will have been based on a number of things: your GCSE results; your AS level and module results at the end of Year 12; your overall performance in the sixth form. Schools are now expert at predicting the right grades for students, so you have to trust them. If schools get it wrong, it is normally because they have made the predictions too high.
- The more popular the degree course you apply for, the higher your predicted grades need to be. For example, English, law, medicine and veterinary science will normally

require AAB (or even higher). If you are not predicted these grades then your application will probably be unsuccessful. Were you realistic when you chose your course?

- Some degree courses, such as chemistry or mechanical engineering, are experiencing a decline in applications and you may have decided to take more of a risk. If the university was looking for BBC and you were predicted CCC you may still have a chance of being made an offer.

Location of the university

All kinds of issues come into play here and it really boils down to personal preference. So how did you decide where you wanted to go?

- Did you think you would prefer a greenfield site, redbrick university or city campus?
- Would you like to go away or be a home student?
- Were you influenced by religious or family issues?
- Was the nearness to or distance from home a deciding factor?
- What about the costs of being a student in a particular city?
- Does the university provide accommodation or do you have to find it yourself?
- Is there a good ratio of male students to female students?
- Are you a supporter of the city's football team?

Reputation of the university

In the past, a university's reputation might have rested pretty much on hearsay. Nowadays, there is more information on which to base a judgement. Superb information is now available through the www.unistats.com website including student satisfaction, the annual entry qualifications that students have for individual courses and graduate employment destinations.

Finally, have you thought carefully about your reasons for wanting to go to university? Sometimes people use university as a means of leaving home, or of delaying going into full-time work. This is fine up to a point. However, we would suggest that, for anyone contemplating a university course, *at least one* of the following points must apply.

- You know your academic strengths (confirmed by exam results or teachers' opinions) and you would like to continue studying a particular subject at university.
- You have a career idea that matches your interests, abilities, values and attitudes.
- You have developed an interest in a new subject that matches your interests, abilities, values and attitudes.

So now let us ask the question again: why have you applied for your course? Hopefully, you have an answer.

2. 'Tell me more about yourself'

As well as questions specifically related to your chosen course, interviewers are highly likely to throw in some more general topics for discussion. In doing so, they are trying to discover more about your personality, your values, your outlook on life and you motivation for doing the course. Here is a list of examples, with some hints from us about how to formulate your answers. Remember: you could be asked some or none of these questions.

At the end of this section you will find some very perceptive comments given by real-life sixth-formers soon after their university interviews. Their advice is worth reading.

Sample interview questions

- Tell us about your school subjects.
- What grades do you expect to get?
- What is your strongest subject?
➤ Make sure you are positive in your answers. If you have found a subject or topic difficult, what steps have you taken to overcome this?

- Why have you applied to this university?
➤ This is your chance to show that you have read the prospectus, looked at the website and visited on the university open day.

- Why have you applied for a deferred entry?
- What plans have you got for your year off?
- If you have had a year off, what did you do and what did you learn from it?
➤ Most admissions tutors will be happy with any gap-year plans, as long as you know what you are going to do, where you are going to do it, when you are going to do it, why you are doing it and who you are doing it with.

- What do you do in your spare time?
- What books do you read?
- What are your musical interests?
- What sports do you like?
- What is the outside interest you would most like to pursue at university?
➤ Please make sure that you reread your personal statement thoroughly, reminding yourself of any points that you might be questioned on.

- How did you become a senior prefect at school and what does it entail?
- How did you get to be assistant editor of your school magazine?
- What did you do for your Duke of Edinburgh's Award/Young Enterprise programme? What did you learn from the experience?
- Tell us about your work experience/part-time job.
➤ Think about how these questions can be related to the course you are applying for.

- What have you got to offer this course?
- Why do you think we should accept you?
- If I made you an offer of AAA, would you be depressed or would you think, 'Go for it!'
- If you were a teacher describing yourself, what would you say?
- What are your qualities and what are your 'bad' points?
- If you have a problem, how do you cope with it?

> Admissions tutors are now fed up with people saying things like, 'I'm enthusiastic, I can work in a team, I have good communication skills,' without any real evidence. Think of examples and evidence (maybe from a part-time job). Otherwise these statements are meaningless.

- Are you ambitious?
- What are your main ambitions?
- What are your career aims?
- What challenges are you looking for?
- Do you have any heroes?

> These questions are intended to discover whether you know where you are going in life and how you are going to get there. Someone who is hopeful about the future will always impress.

- What do you think about student loans and student finance generally?
- Will you be living in halls or at home?

> Be honest, but try to see all sides of the issue.

Students' comments

- 'The man who showed us round the department turned out to be the interviewer, so you have to be conscious of making a good impression *all* the time.'

- 'Make sure you can justify/defend *everything* you put in UCAS Apply.'

- 'It's important to be properly prepared. I made a list of all the possible questions I would be asked and how to answer them. I also made a list of all the questions I could ask about the course – number of teachers, types of projects, etc.'

- 'I had developed some outline answers in my mind, which were very useful, but I'm glad I didn't go into the interview room with a set of stock memorized answers to a set of stock questions. I was asked questions I wasn't quite expecting and I was asked questions from a different angle to how I was expecting.'

- 'My interviews might have gone badly if I hadn't prepared some questions of my own to ask, as the very first thing they asked me was, "Have you got any questions?"'

- 'It's good to know a bit about the college/university and course beforehand. For example, I was asked a question about social anthropology, which I was prepared for because I knew it was the tutor's research area (you can look in the course prospectus or at the relevant university or college website).'

- 'They didn't ask me about things I hadn't learnt at school. They didn't try to catch me out. Or if they did it was too subtle for me to notice!'

- 'After having had five Cambridge interviews I can quite confidently say that they are not as daunting as you might expect.'

- 'He was very hostile when I walked in. He sat with his feet on the desk, chewing gum, throughout the interview.'

- 'The phone rang in the middle.'

- 'I think that the hostile interviewer was just trying to put me under pressure to see how I would react.'

- 'The panel did not look up once. They simply took notes and made no comment to my answers. At the end they told me they had many people to see, so they interrupted me as I was answering a question and asked me to leave. So I was really surprised to get an offer of CCC. The interview was dreadful and I was expecting a rejection.'

- 'I arrived slightly late due to transport problems but they didn't seem to mind. It did, however, put me ill at ease and I was somewhat disorientated as I was called for interview as soon as I arrived. This should be avoided at all costs!'

- 'The people interviewing you are the cleverest in the world. There's no point trying to trick them by pretending to have read books you haven't – they personally know the authors!'

- 'Never pretend you have nice intelligent hobbies such as art or stamp collecting – these guys are experts on everything.'

- 'As I was leaving the room one of the interviewers wanted a sheet of paper back from me and held out her hand. Embarrassingly, I shook it. So there goes my place then!'

- 'Don't be worried if everyone around you seems like a brain in a jar – it's not all they're looking for (I hope)!'

- 'There was a 20 minute group interview during a half-day open day with a friendly and opinionated interviewer. It was hinted throughout we would get offers. Very few people get individual interviews (for this course) and we were told the interviewed candidates were seen because they weren't of such a high calibre.'

3. 'Is there anything you'd like to ask?'

At some point in the interview you will probably be asked if you have any questions. Sometimes this will come at the end of the interview. Some interviewers, however, will make it an integral part of the conversation and the question may come quite early on. The important thing is not to ask a question just for the sake of it. Only ask something you really want to know the answer to.

You will probably have questions about the content and structure of the course (read the prospectus carefully). If these have not already been covered during the interview, then ask.

In addition, here are some ideas for you to think about. Information about the following areas is not always included in prospectuses or departmental brochures and so may form a basis for your questions.

- The career prospects for graduates.
- The opportunities for post-graduate research.
- The study facilities. (Is the course taught on a single site? Is there a departmental library?)
- The way the course is taught. (Are there lectures, seminars or tutorials and what size are the groups?)
- The personal support for students. (Is there a personal tutor system?)
- The placements for sandwich courses. (How are they organized? Who is responsible for finding the placement?)
- The accommodation situation.
- The possibility of meeting some students currently on the course.

4. Personal preparation and presentation

Points to remember

- The fact that you have been invited for an interview means that the university is interested in you, so that is half your battle won.
- In any interview, as in any conversation, there should be a two-way interaction. Make sure you participate and contribute.
- An interview can last anything between ten minutes and an hour.
- Interviews are usually conducted by one interviewer, but there could be two, three or even four of them.
- There is no such thing as the perfect interview.

Preparation

- Read carefully any material that is sent to you before the interview, so that you know what to expect when you get there.
- Re-read the university prospectus and details about the course.
- Photocopy or print off your personal statement and re-read this thoroughly before the interview.
- Prepare some questions you may want to ask (see previous chapter). Make sure they have not already been answered in information you have been sent by the university.
- Plan your journey. If an overnight stay is involved, plan for this as well. Do *not* be late or in a rush.

Presentation

- If you are applying for a vocational degree (for example, medicine or hotel management) it is usually best to err on the side of convention and dress smartly and appropriately.
- For most degrees, dress in clothing that you feel comfortable with, and that will not distract the interviewer from the points you want to make.
- Do *not* chew gum – whatever course you are applying for!
- Think about what your body language is conveying. Do *not* sit slumped in your seat wearing a baseball cap! It is important to engage with the interviewer from the start.
- When it comes to handshakes, sitting down, starting to talk, and so on, take your lead from the interviewer.
- Work on making eye contact, regulating your voice levels and putting across an appropriate level of friendliness and warmth.

5. Applying for medicine

This section has been written by Harriet Nerva who attended La Swap Sixth Form Consortium and is now at Liverpool Medical School. It was written in April 2008 and is based on her own experiences and research. All opinions expressed are Harriet's. We would like to thank to her for such a superb contribution produced in her own time.

See also the Medicine section under 'A-Z of university subjects.'

Introduction

This brief guide looks at how you can maximise your chances of securing a place at a medical school. It covers:

- The quirks that nobody tells you about when you choose your four places.
- The perils of predictions - when is the best time for YOU to apply?
- Essential reading.
- The importance of work experience.
- Interviews.

When I applied to medical school I had little idea of the **huge amount** of time and energy I would devote to getting a place. Medicine is tough, and so is the application process. With over 20,000 applicants chasing around 7,000 places, the process should be approached like a military operation requiring strategy and planning and, of course, a large dose of your precious sixth form time.

Do not underestimate how much time it will take you to prepare everything you need in your application. One medical school used to list several attributes that it saw as ensuring successful applicants were "excellent in every respect": Students needed to have been a school prefect, played at least two musical instruments, be fluent in at least two languages, played for their county, and held a number of Duke of Edinburgh awards - all in addition to strong A levels (no jokes!). The admissions process for medicine is no longer run like this, but the sentiment still holds true.

Choosing your four places

Along with producing a good UCAS Apply and personal statement, making effective and **realistic** choices of medical school greatly increases your chances of a place.

What to consider:
- The type of course
- The location
- Entry requirements

- The university itself

The type of course
The main differences in the type of course involve the style of teaching and how early clinical exposure begins. The latter is an important factor to consider. Some applicants really want to be able to apply their scientific knowledge from early on in a clinical context. Whilst medical schools are now encouraged to introduce clinical experience in the early years, there are a diverse range of courses. The words "early clinical exposure" mean different things to different universities.

Some background
Until 1994 most medical schools ran traditional courses which involved three years of academic study of medical science (pre-clinical stage) and then two/three years of clinical exposure, with students gaining experience in hospital. The pre-clinical years had quite a rigid format with the different disciplines (anatomy, physiology, pharmacology) being taught separately.

In 1993 the GMC published *Tomorrow's Doctors*, a new initiative to improve and update medical undergraduate teaching to the next millennium. Its principal recommendations included a reduction in the burden of factual information for undergraduates, a promotion of learning core material and the encouragement of learning through curiosity. The latter has led to the introduction of supplementary study options schemes in most medical schools.

An emphasis was to be placed on the teaching of communication skills and public health medicine. In addition, attitudes of mind and behaviour that befit a doctor were to be inculcated and the divide between preclinical and clinical studies was to be bridged by a systems based curriculum and early contact with patients. The response to the report has been varied across medical schools.

Traditional
Oxford and Cambridge still have traditional courses. Preclinical and clinical medicine is taught separately at Oxbridge. All undergraduate pre-clinical students read for a BA on completing their first 3 years of study. The preclinical course will give you a very strong grounding in the medical sciences. You are essentially studying for a science degree and patient contact is minimal.

Integrated
The majority of medical schools have adopted an integrated course. Courses are usually systems-based (e.g. cardiovascular, digestive) rather than discipline-based so you are learning material in a more holistic manner. The general trend is towards lectures and tutorials in the first couple of years, with formalised en masse teaching being replaced by ward-based teaching later in the course. Clinical exposure in the first years is often taken to be visits to GPs and clinics and nothing more.

Universities with integrated courses include: Edinburgh, UCL, Leeds, Nottingham, Birmingham, Newcastle, Durham, Brighton and Sussex and Bristol.

If early clinical exposure is important to you, do check out exactly what the course is offering and talk to current medical students. At one university open day I was told that early clinical exposure was a key feature, only to be told later by a medical student there that there was really very little of it!

Problem based learning (PBL)

According to the BMA: 'In problem based learning (PBL) students use "triggers" from the problem case or scenario to define their own learning objectives. Subsequently they do independent, self-directed study before returning to the group to discuss and refine their acquired knowledge. Thus, PBL is not about problem solving per se, but rather it uses appropriate problems to increase knowledge and understanding. The process is clearly defined, and the several variations that exist all follow a similar series of steps.'[1]

Step 1—Identify and clarify unfamiliar terms presented in the scenario; scribe lists those that remain unexplained after discussion
Step 2—Define the problem or problems to be discussed; students may have different views on the issues, but all should be considered; scribe records a list of agreed problems
Step 3—"Brainstorming" session to discuss the problem(s), suggesting possible explanations on basis of prior knowledge; students draw on each other's knowledge and identify areas of incomplete knowledge; scribe records all discussion
Step 4—Review steps 2 and 3 and arrange explanations into tentative solutions; scribe organises the explanations and restructures if necessary
Step 5—Formulate learning objectives; group reaches consensus on the learning objectives; tutor ensures learning objectives are focused, achievable, comprehensive, and appropriate
Step 6—Private study (all students gather information related to each learning objective)
Step 7—Group shares results of private study (students identify their learning resources and share their results); tutor checks learning and may assess the group

Students are split into groups and meet three or four times a week to discuss one clinical scenario. The group, helped by a facilitator, will decide on learning objectives for that case (scientific knowledge, ethics, public health, statistics) and each student will do independent learning and then return to discuss what they have found. Students are not left to their own devices entirely as there are lectures (but significantly fewer than on integrated courses) and clinical skills and communication sessions. As PBL courses rely on lots and lots of independent work self-motivation and dedication to the course are extremely important. This approach is not for everybody.

Examples of PBL courses: Liverpool, Glasgow, QMUL, Manchester, and East Anglia (very PBL heavy).

---

[1] From the ABC of learning and teaching medicine: Problem based learning
http://www.bmj.com/cgi/reprint/326/7384/328.pdf

Advantages of PBL

- Student-centred—It fosters active learning, improved understanding, and retention and development of lifelong learning skills.
- Generic competencies—PBL allows students to develop generic skills and attitudes desirable in their future practice.
- Integration—PBL facilitates an integrated core curriculum.
- Motivation—PBL is fun for students and tutors, and the process requires all students to be engaged in the learning process.
- "Deep" learning—PBL fosters deep learning (students interact with learning materials, relate concepts to everyday activities, and improve their understanding).
- Constructivist approach—Students activate prior knowledge and build on existing conceptual knowledge frameworks.

Disadvantages of PBL

- Tutors who do not get a chance to "teach"—Tutors enjoy passing on their own knowledge and understanding so may find PBL facilitation difficult and frustrating.
- Human resources—More staff have to take part in the tutoring process.
- Other resources—Large numbers of students need access to the same library and computer resources simultaneously.
- Role models—Students may be deprived access to a particular inspirational teacher who, in a traditional curriculum, would deliver lectures to a large group.
- Information overload—Students may be unsure how much self-directed study to do and what information is relevant and useful.

When to apply – year 13 vs. post-A level application

Yes medicine is a long haul – why defer a year and apply post-A level? Well consider the following – **it may make all the difference to you.**

Predictions

In order to be considered by the medical school you need to have strong predictions, and as the medical schools can often see your AS results from your UCAS Apply, if these are not up to scratch, the medical school is most unlikely to interview you. If your AS grades (particularly in biology and chemistry) are low for medicine, or on the border of grades, it is seriously worth thinking about deferring.

My experience: My AS-Levels were good but, in terms of medicine, the marks were just a bit too low for my school to predict for me the grades required. I took a decision there and then to defer and apply a year later. I went on to achieve three As.

Other advantages of applying post A Level

- You are applying with your grades - the university has no risk that you might not get your grades – you are therefore automatically a more attractive proposition.
- Some universities want AAB, some want AAA, and some want As in particular subjects. If you apply with your grades you know where to apply and where not to, so you do not waste any of your four choices.
- You will generally have more time to research current medical issues.
- You will have less stress in Year 13 and more time to devote to your studies. Interviews and post-offer open days take a lot of preparation and time away from A Level studies.
- There will be more time to consider if medicine is for you. Once you hit 18 there are more healthcare roles available to you and more scope for good work experience. Remember you can't volunteer in the NHS under age 18.
- *You will stick out - most people apply in Year 13. Ask your referee to explain in your reference that you applied a year later to make sure that medicine was right for you and you will appear mature and level headed. Or put it in your personal statement.*

Disadvantages of applying post A Level
- You will have to take a gap year.
- Applying can place constraints on your gap year. Interviews can take place anywhere from November to April and sometimes you will not be given as little as a week's notice. Many universities give all offers and rejections at the end of the application cycle in March which feels like a drag. Many of your friends will nearly have finished their first year at university by then!
- It can be lonely if your friends are either at university or abroad on a gap year and you are at home waiting for medical school interviews and offers.

Entry Requirements

At the time of writing some medical schools have increased entry requirements from AAB to AAA. Most are still asking for at least AAB with chemistry being compulsory and most preferring biology as well.

Having said this, there are often many variations in medical school entry requirements, and some of these are not always obvious at first sight.

In a bid to select candidates from an ever-increasing pool, many medical schools now ask for a specific level of GCSE attainment, so this is definitely worth keeping an eye out for. Some medical school discriminate on the number of A* grades at GCSE - a criterion that will seem unfair to those with 3 A grade A levels but insufficient A* at GCSEs.

Some examples of different grade and subject criteria (as of 2007) to bear in mind when choosing your medical schools:

Criteria	Medical Schools
Require high number of A* GCSEs	Edinburgh and Birmingham (7A*+)
Does not require chemistry A Level	East Anglia
Require an A in both biology and chemistry	Liverpool, Nottingham
Do not interview	Edinburgh and Southampton
Do not require biology as second science (but do require one of biology, physics or maths as a second science)	Aberdeen, Birmingham, Dundee, Edinburgh, Glasgow, Keele, Leeds, Manchester, Newcastle, Oxford, Peninsula, Sheffield
Requires subjects with no lower than 60% theoretical content	Manchester (this rules out music, art, IT, DT etc.)
Requires 3 sciences at AS level	Sheffield
Do not require UKCAT	Liverpool, Bristol
Prefers applicants with a 3rd non-science A Level	UCL

You should check the latest criteria before making your choice.

A word of warning: **do not use university websites solely for your research as they are often not updated.** For example, I found one medical school's website saying that a minimum of 4 A*s at GCSE was required. However on phoning them to check I was told that 7 to 8 A*s were needed (which I took to mean 8 A*s – I only have 6 so too bad). **Telephone them.**

Useful resources

The Insiders' Guide to UK Medical Schools published by BMA books and updated annually. This is a very helpful book which gets current students at every medical school to give the detailed low-down on their course, location and university. It also contains all application entry data from the previous year.

www.newmediamedicine.com/forum is a lively forum used by applicants, students and doctors with lots of questions and answers on each medical school. A lot of applicants discuss their interviews and offers/rejections on here.

www.thestudentroom.co.uk has another of these forums.

For the UKCAT:
Passing the UK Clinical Aptitude Test (UKCAT) and BMAT (Student Guides to University Entrance) (Paperback) by Felicity Taylor, Rosalie Hutton and Glenn Hutton (Author).

Contains practice questions and hints on the UKCAT. It's expensive but will give you piece of mind because, although it's hard to practise for the UKCAT, at least you will know what to expect. It also has a good section on the application process generally.

For the BMAT:
Preparing for the BMAT: The Official Guide to the BioMedical Admissions Test (Paperback) by John Butterworth and Geoff Thwaites

Getting an interview vs. getting a place: the odds

Looking at application statistics (see *The Insiders' Guide to Medical School,* cited above), at many places the chances of getting a place increases (in some places quite dramatically) once you have an interview. For example, some medical schools receive 10 applicants for every place but they interview 3 applicants for every place and make 2 offers for every place. This shows how your odds increase dramatically if you break through to interview.

The other thing to remember is that whereas you may get more than one stab at an interview and you can do lots of interview practice, you will only write one personal statement so it is important that you really focus on it.

Whilst everyone's personal statement should be different, here are some pointers to think about (in no order):

- Why medicine? Probably the hardest thing to write about without sounding corny. Try not to sound too trite by writing about helping people and do not write that you have wanted to be a doctor since the age of three, or since your sister had her tonsils removed. Instead you might focus on what you could bring to medicine and what really inspires you about it. Many use this bit as an opener for their statement.

- You can show how your extra-curricular activities have given you the qualities needed for medicine. Selectors like to hear about your teamwork and communication skills and are keen to see that you have contributed to your local community (e.g. your school). Many applicants seem to talk about their A Level subjects as a basis for their interest in medicine, but as nearly everyone else is studying sciences, it can be hard to stand out.

- Work experience - briefly say what you did and then discuss what you learnt. It is also useful to try and link this to your interests. When I wrote my personal statement I mentioned how I was very interested to see that there was a possible link between mental illness and diabetes, based on my month working as a volunteer nursing assistant on a psychiatric ward. I commented on how I talked to doctors about this and did a bit of my own research (on the net only).

- You seem to be expected to have an idea of an area of medicine that interests you and you should be prepared to be probed on this at interview as evidence of why you are applying for medicine. This is NOT about a committing yourself at this stage to a speciality. It is about showing an informed interest and it is much easier to write and discuss this if you can draw on actual experience. **Which is why work experience is so important.**

Work Experience

Most medical schools like to see that you have some exposure to the healthcare system, be it through shadowing staff, volunteering or working. By doing work experience you are showing that you are really committed to studying medicine.

Medical schools are keen to see that you understand:

- How the doctor fits into the wider multi-disciplinary team (learn this phrase, it crops up a lot!)
- What dilemmas a doctor may face in day to day treatment (ethical questions)
- The advantages and disadvantages of medicine.

Getting work experience is not easy. School will help you to some degree. However, you have to remember that you cannot volunteer in the NHS under the age of 18 which means that you may find, especially if your birthday is in the second half of the academic year, that its very hard to fit in work experience with studying.

This leaves volunteering in the community, most commonly in old people's homes. This will show you are caring and will give you an insight into being old, but may not put you at the coalface of healthcare. Try your local Volunteer Bureau – there is a national network.

All hospitals run temporary nursing staff banks (like an internal temporary staff agency) which take on unqualified people to do locum shifts as nursing assistants and you can also try to volunteer through the nursing bank. However note that this takes a long time to arrange because you need Criminal Record Bureau checks and to have had Hepatitis B jabs which take 8 months minimum. So you need to plan this a year before you want to do the work and if your birthday is at the end of the year it may be a factor to take into account when you consider when to apply (see above). Many hospitals have volunteer bureaux and you can obtain details from Trust websites. Again you need to allow time for all the forms and checks to be done.

Being a (volunteer) nursing assistant is a great way to understand how the multi-disciplinary team works and its respective roles. You are almost a fly on the wall and you may even be asked to contribute in a ward round about one of the patients.

Do use your contacts. My GP arranged for me to go to another practice locally for a week where I did some administrative work behind reception and shadowed a health visitor. Ask him/her to introduce you to a hospital consultant in a specialty that you are interested in and ask to shadow them.

One thing I found out: **all the doctors I met loved to help young would-be doctors.**

Medicine Taster Courses

Opinion is divided on how productive medicine taster programmes like *Medlink* and *Medsin* are. Based at a university campus (usually at Nottingham University) for 4-5 days, in the winter and spring holidays and aimed at sixth form students, these programmes claim to be:

"valuable for students in years 12 and 13, as not only will they hear guidance on applying to medical school but also on what to do if things go wrong and they need to reapply. Advice on surviving medical school will be given by medical students, and everyone will have the opportunity to talk with practising doctors and medical students, in addition to the opportunity of meeting face to face with the majority of the country's medical schools admission tutors during the Medlink Exhibition." (From the Medlink Website)

I went on Medlink in December 2005 when I was in Year 12. The range of talks by different doctors and medical students were quite informative and I did get the chance to size up the opposition and get a flavour of university life.

However, these programmes are incredibly expensive and you have to pay for absolutely every extra (including food), which did make it feel like one big money-making exercise. Although they claim to give you lots of help with your personal statement, this help was pretty minimal.

Some people mention their attendance at one of these courses on their personal statement, but with at least 2,000 delegates attending the courses in total, your attendance will not stand out and there is only so much you can say about it. I saw it as something that would give me information and help me to make a decision on whether medicine was right for me rather than something that I would put on my personal statement to prove my commitment to medicine.

So, to sum up, it's useful, but in no way essential, to your application.

For further information on the programmes, please see the website www.medlink-uk.com. If you would like to book a place, make sure that you do so early (August/September) as places book up quickly.

Your Reference

A helpful guide to references from the University of Manchester Medical School. Can be found at: www.medicine.manchester.ac.uk/undergraduate/medicine/applying/reference.

Ask to see your reference and make sure it is totally consistent with your personal statement and reinforces the way you are trying to present yourself.

This means that you must give your referee a copy of your personal statement and allow plenty of time for a number of drafts. Given that the deadline for applying for medicine is the middle of October, you should be working with your referee from early September. Remember: your personal statement and the reference should reflect each other.

The Interview Process

I had four interviews (and three offers), each one very different in style and content. However in all of them I found myself drawing heavily on my work experience. Sometimes I was asked directly about what I had done but, more often, I used my experience to illustrate the points I was trying to make.

Some medical schools think that it is fairest to use a standardised pre-set list of questions for all candidates, such as the one below. This means that you will not be asked directly about your personal statement and you have to weave it into your answers. However, in one interview all that we talked about was my personal statement.

The website www.medical-interviews.co.uk/Resources/QuestionsMS.htm lists over 150 questions under the following headings:
1. Background & Motivation for Medicine
2. Knowledge of The Medical School
3. Depth & Breadth of Interest in Medicine
4. Team Work
5. Personal Insight
6. Understanding of The Role of Medicine in Society
7. Work Experience
8. Tolerance of Ambiguity & Ethics

Here is a list of pre-set questions that I was asked at one interview:
- Why do you want to be a doctor?
- Tell us about what steps you have taken to clarify why medicine
- What other voluntary work have you done?
- Tell us about a situation when you had to take responsibility
- What would you do if you were part of the clinical team and a doctor kept coming in late for work and kept blaming it on the traffic?
- A question about inequalities in healthcare
- A question on hobbies

Thus, as you can see, your work experience is not just about showing that you are caring and motivated. It should also give you a greater understanding of health and social care issues, and something to talk about at interview. **The message is to choose your work experience carefully.**

Most medical schools (bar Oxbridge) will not ask questions of an academic nature. However, they will expect you to have a basic understanding of the some of the ideas underpinning modern medicine. You may be asked directly about these ideas and should refer to them when discussing medical issues and ethical problems.

These topics may include:
- The four principles of medicine
- The Hippocratic Oath
- Basic structure of the NHS and its workings (including the General Medical Council and the British Medical Association)
- The training path of a doctor
- The concept of capacity

In addition:
- You need to have a medical discovery/advance that you think is important ready to discuss (I discussed the impact of day care surgery developed in the 1950s).
- You need to have thought through ethical issues including abortion, euthanasia, fertility treatment and 'who gets the organ' style scenarios.
- You need to have a current health news issue ready to talk about.
- You need to be prepared to talk about anything which you have written on your personal statement.

Useful resources for the interview process:
Medical School Interviews: A Practical Guide to Help You Get That Place at Medical School - Over 150 Questions Analysed by George Lee and Olivier Picard.

This is a very useful paperback. As the title says, the book analyses over 150 questions and really tells you about the pitfalls to avoid. It gives you lots of ideas for your own answers and goes through some important ideas and terms, such as the meaning of capacity and the four principles of medicine.

www.medschoolsonline.co.uk

news.bbc.co.uk/1/hi/health very good for a quick summary of up to date health news

www.guardian.co.uk/health blogs provide a wide range of views from the general public on health topics. Interesting set of special reports on health and social care

www.bmj.com and www.student.bmj.com to remind you what you're letting yourself in for.

Last Word

I wrote this guide on my gap year following the end of the interview cycle 2008 and I am off to Liverpool University in September 2008. Over my sixth form years I amassed a lot of information on medical schools and I hope this information is useful.

Good luck!

Harriet Nerva
La Swap Sixth Form Consortium 2005 to 2007
Liverpool Medical School entrant Sept 2008

6. A realistic application to Oxbridge

Never, in the history of education, has so much hot air been wasted on a single issue. Rather than adding to the global warming attributable to this subject, this is our attempt to deconstruct what is really going on. It is written presuming the reader is a teacher or careers adviser who has recently been given responsibility for students who might be considering an Oxbridge application.

A framework to help your students

A helpful acronym

In careers guidance, if we are trying to make something more understandable, our first tactic is to create an acronym. This will hopefully remind you of the issues you need to be aware of to help your possible Oxbridge applicants:

G	–	Grades
R	–	Reading
I	–	Interview
S	–	Subject
T	–	Tests

The phrase 'grist to the mill' refers to turning something to one's profit or advantage. Turning the resources available in the sixth form to the student's advantage is exactly what is required for a successful Oxbridge application and is what will be addressed in this section.

Grades

We need to ensure that possible candidates have a realistic idea of what GCSE, AS and A Level (or equivalent qualification) grades or scores are typical of a successful Oxbridge applicant and that they receive this information in time to act on it. Some would argue that by being specific about grades we could be putting off talented potential applicants. We would disagree. In practice we need clarity, not ambiguity.

- Typical GCSE grades

Both Cambridge and Oxford are now openly saying that the average applicant has 5-8 A*s at GCSE. Moreover, Cambridge is saying that even if the applicant has been to a challenging school they normally have 3-4 A*s - and quite often more. There can be exceptions, but the person doing the reference must be prepared to give comparative evidence as to why the student is an exception and refer to compensatory and contextual factors.

- Typical AS grades

Getting A grades at AS Level is not normally enough. For Cambridge they need to be high AS grades, with applicants having 87-92% UMS scores in their three most relevant or best subjects. Oxford seems to be placing more emphasis on the performance in tests (see below) though in reality their applicants will have similar UMS scores. Please remember that Cambridge applicants have to declare their AS Level UMS scores on the on-line supplementary form.

- Typical A Level grades

AAA will be the norm (including the expected prediction). If you want a real eye-opener, check UCAS Tariff scores for Oxford and Cambridge degrees in www.unistats.com. At the time of writing it is too early to make reference to the use of the A* grade in offers. The first A Level results including the A* will come out in August 2010. University prospectuses coming out in March 2011 could be enlightening.

When writing a reference for an applicant you should place his or her academic ability in the context of where they stand in comparison to the rest of the year group. Any other contextual information could also be usefully added.

Reading

Possible applicants need to understand that they will have to read more widely than for most other university interviews, be prepared to analyse what they have read and offer a critique. Some students may need help with choosing texts or, in maths and the sciences, practising problems. The more they read and do that is related to their subject the more they will have to say in their personal statement.

It is essential:
- That the student learns that without wider reading or subject related activity they will have very little evidence to back up their claim to be interested and engaged in their subject.

- That the student understands how the admissions tutor is likely to look for salient points in the personal statement as possible embarkation points for deeper questioning in the interview.

- That he or she learns that anything that is put in the statement can lead to a question which may be followed up with others on the same topic.

- That the student learns to talk and discuss issues with friends, teachers and family.

The importance of critical and analytical reading beyond the confines of an A Level syllabus cannot be stressed enough.

Interview

It is crucial that possible applicants are given tasks:
- Which give them experience of dealing with subject-based questions and how they need to engage in the interview (By engage, we mean answering questions that arise from the answers they gave to the original question from the interviewer).

- Which make them think for themselves rather than regurgitate what they have been taught by a teacher.

- Which make them realise that they need to understand fully what each of them has written in his or her personal statement, a copy of which must be kept to refer to ahead of interviews. In addition they must understand that not being able to talk at length about what they have written is likely to be interpreted as a lack of motivation or commitment.

- Which help them to learn how admissions tutors will focus upon salient points in the statement as possible topics to bring up.

- Which try to replicate the interview experience. Applicants should have a mock interview, preferably with someone who is knowledgeable on the subject and whom they do not know well. They should also watch videos produced by, for example, Oriel College Oxford, Oxford Learning Institute and Emmanuel College Cambridge to gain a clearer understanding of the interview process.

We feel very strongly that applicants, especially from non-selective state schools, will often have no experience of being interrogated on an academic issue. They may answer questions in class but they will not normally have had to face further questioning on their original answer. All applicants must be exposed to appropriate questioning related to their subject in a mock interview scenario. A useful way of looking at an Oxbridge interview is as "an exam paper out loud." Once applicants have an awareness of what the interview experience will be like, they should put their efforts into wider reading around their subject. This is much more important than doing repeated mock interviews.

Subject

Candidates need to understand why they are applying for their chosen subject. Mainly the subject should relate to their abilities and interests, but it could also relate to their values (politics for example). Obsessive enthusiasm backed by evidence of serious interest is the only way forward here. One Oxford tutor has told us with 'due humour' that in this context "geekiness is good!"

Students need to understand that they will mainly be asked subject-based questions, with the possible starting points being:
- Something extracted from the personal statement
- A piece of marked work (possibly in a different subject than that for which they are applying to study)
- Something that has been covered in the A Level syllabus but which is then extended and developed. This type of questioning is intended to test how students can think for themselves and how they can apply their existing knowledge to new situations.

Tests

Potential applicants need to know that they may have to take additional tests either at school or at the interview and they need to have experience of being exposed to what is involved.

They may face a formal test (the Oxford or Cambridge thinking skills assessment (TSA), English literature admissions test (ELAT), biomedical admissions test (BMAT), Sixth Term Examination Paper (STEP), LNAT: the national admissions test for law, history aptitude test (HAT)) or an informal test (an unseen poem, some text in a foreign language, a scientific problem, a piece of historical text). Overall, Oxford seems to have more formal tests whereas Cambridge has more informal tests and also wants more in-depth information on AS Level performance.

Students need to familiarize themselves with the content and style of any formal tests and be informed of the relevant website details. We feel it is important that students are given the formal tests in a mock exam situation and, where possible, that their answers are marked so they have a realistic idea of how they did. All the websites for the above tests have examples of past/sample papers.

The student should practise dealing with related unfamiliar texts, articles or problems even if they do not face a formal test. There may well be an informal test at interview.

Contextual issues and student background

All the above presumes that the applicant has, of their own free will, decided that they want to apply for an Oxford or Cambridge college. It does not try to deal with the wider issues of encouraging students to apply to Oxbridge. Nor does it address the perceived social injustices of the education system which Oxford and Cambridge universities are often accused of maintaining. Please do not confuse the applicant with the sociology of education issues that often come up in the media relating to Oxbridge application. These issues will be irrelevant to the applicant and will divert them from the GRIST framework.

Other issues such as college choice, understanding the Cambridge supervision system, the Oxford tutorial system and finding out contextual information that can be passed on to the Cambridge and Oxford colleges, should be covered with possible applicants. But we would argue that they are not as important as the above issues in the GRIST framework. See 'Other points to consider' below.

Many organisations offer to help improve an applicant's chance of getting into Oxbridge. They often charge fees and you should be aware of the danger of over-preparation. We would argue that all they are doing is implementing elements of the GRIST framework, which can be done at a school or local authority level with the support of Oxford and Cambridge Universities themselves. We would also argue that Oxford and Cambridge Universities methods of selections are as fair, or in fact fairer, than other common selection processes used by other universities, as they use a wider range of methods to make their final selection. HOWEVER, one obvious weakness in the Oxbridge and Cambridge Universities' methods of selection is that there is not "equality of preparation". This clearly varies between schools and areas. It is therefore for schools, local authorities and Oxbridge themselves, to help implement the GRIST framework and work towards "equality of preparation". To be fair, Oxford and Cambridge Universities do recognise this criticism and adjust their approaches accordingly.

Other points to consider

What makes Oxford and Cambridge Universities different?
- The quality of the educational experience. Students will often be taught by the 'leaders in their fields' and, in return, they will have to push themselves to achieve very high levels of work. It should not be forgotten that there is, of course, academic excellence at other universities as well.
- More teaching is done individually. Students are expected to be self-starters and work independently.
- Whatever the degree, Oxbridge graduates have very good career prospects. A certain level of respect from employers is gained simply because of the university attended (though this effect diminishes over time).
- Colleges are normally friendly places, in pleasant surroundings. Accommodation provision is often very good.
- Oxbridge colleges still have a better level of funding than other universities.

What potential candidates need to know about the college system
- Oxford University and Cambridge University each have over 20 colleges. Students should not be put off by some idiosyncratic pronunciations. Magdalene College, for example, is pronounced *maud-lin*.
- Lectures are taught by the university. English lectures, for example, will be taught at the university's English faculty.
- Tutorials (at Oxford) and supervisions (at Cambridge) involve being taught individually or in small groups at the student's own college.
- Undergraduates live, eat and socialize at their colleges, in the main.
- Cambridge colleges, on the whole, will find accommodation for three years. Oxford colleges vary. Some will ask students to go into the private rented sector in the second year.
- It is unusual for two people from the same school to apply for the same subject at the same college.

Points for students to consider when choosing a college at Oxbridge
- Does the college offer accommodation for the duration of the course?
- Does the college have a fellow or director of studies in the relevant subject?
- Students should research the college that interests them most, but not become too attached. Applications may be pooled and an offer come from another college.
- *Students cannot apply to both Oxford and Cambridge.*

Preparing for interview? A Cambridge Admissions Tutor's perspective

From: *Admissions to Higher Education: Advisers' Directory*, published by the Specialist Schools & Academies Trust

UCAS personal statement

Admissions tutors use these to tell them about the appropriateness of an applicant's chosen subject and course, and suitable embarkation-points for discussion at interview. Subject focus is therefore vital, as is an account of any reading and/or other wider subject exploration that has been completed; this might include work experience for vocational courses. Applicants who overly gild the lily in their personal statements are likely to be found out badly at interview, so honesty is crucial. Extra-curricular activities/positions of responsibility might be turned to in the final paragraph of a personal statement, but these matter much less to admissions tutors than is often supposed and therefore the bulk of the personal statement should be focused on the applicant's relationship with his/her chosen subject and with academic study.

Submitted work

Submitted work, where requested, is used to assess an applicant's academic and intellectual ability, and his/her ability to communicate on the page. It is also often used as an embarkation-point for discussion at interview. Which essays work best? If school/college work is requested, it is generally a good idea to send in work very recently completed, as students are developing so fast at this stage in their lives. Applicants should take a copy of anything sent in, so that it can be looked over in advance of interview, should interviews form part of the selection procedure.

Interviews

These are now conducted principally by Oxford, Cambridge and UCL, and by certain medical and law schools, but many selective universities interview some of their applicants. Interviews tend to last 20-45 minutes and are conducted by lecturers. They are predominantly academic and subject-focused.

What do interviewers look for?
- Genuine subject interest
- Appropriateness of chosen course
- Enthusiasm for complex and challenging ideas
- Clarity of thought and analytical ability
- Intellectual flexibility
- Vocational or professional commitment (where appropriate)

What else do you need to know about them?
- They are a discussion in which assessors hope to see applicants thinking problems through for themselves
- They are structured but relatively informal

- Interviewers have no hidden agenda, and do not ask 'trick' questions or erect 'hurdles' for applicants to jump over
- They are not looking for a 'smooth' or 'confident' performance

What to expect
- Focused and challenging questions, typical of teaching and learning at a top university

Applicants are usually asked to talk about:

- Academic work completed in the last year or two
- Relevant wider reading or work experience
- Subject-related issues that are very readily visible in the wider world
- New approaches to existing knowledge

And they are asked to engage with

- Problem-solving questions

Interviews also usually allow applicants to ask questions of the interviewers; a good deal of intervention in discussion, or 'prompting', from the latter is usually a good, not a bad, sign.

Basic preparation for interview
Interviewees should do some 'homework' on:
- Their chosen course
- Their recent school/college work – know your syllabus
- Their UCAS personal statement
- Any submitted essays

It is amazing how many interviewees attend having done none, and therefore struggle for things to talk about.

How should students approach wider exploration? The best way is to read, but valuable exploration can also be done via TV and radio documentaries, via the internet, by attending open lectures or events, by visiting sites or places or interest and, where appropriate, through work experience. Most importantly, students need to **think** about what they explore. The balance between the various means of exploration will vary by individual, opportunity and, most importantly, chosen course.

Arts subjects: reading conventional books and journals (e.g. *History Today*); attending open lectures/events; visiting relevant sites/places
Social science subjects: as above, but with a greater emphasis upon contemporary events and print and electronic media; prominent national or international issues clearly related to an applicant's chosen university subject should be kept up with

Sciences: reading, beyond scientific periodicals like *New Scientist*, is likely to be less important, but popular science in the media should be keenly followed; additional A level units, in, for instance, mathematics, might be completed

Vocational subjects: some work experience is usually important

Interview practice

This is by no means essential; far more important is completing wider exploration and getting used to being analytical and discursive about one's chosen subject. But a practice interview can help build confidence and allay nerves. To have real value, it must be based around subject-focused problem-solving, just like real university interviews. Advice on how to sit, maintaining eye-contact and/or other aspects of 'interview technique' is near to useless; academics are simply not assessing these things. What can really help applicants is being asked challenging, subject-related questions by very friendly but slightly intimidating subject specialists, such as senior teachers/lecturers from their own school/college whom they do not know well, or teachers/lecturers from a neighbouring school/college. Successfully completing twenty minutes of problem-solving in physics should certainly help build the confidence of an engineering applicant, for instance.

On the day

Applicants should dress comfortably; they do not need to wear a suit. Turning up on time and in the right place is essential. They should listen to all questions carefully and feel free to take time to think. In answering, they should try to be clear and focused; they might explain their thought processes as they go. If they realize they have just contradicted a point they themselves made earlier, or that they have got something wrong, they should immediately say so; such recognition is a good sign for interviewers. It is important to concentrate on the current question and not worry about any perceived earlier mistakes; interviews are assessed positively, not negatively, so applicants will not generally be 'marked down'. They should feel free to ask questions or for clarification at any time; nor should they worry about hesitating or getting stuck; content, not style, is what matters. They should have the confidence in their own opinions and ideas, so long as they are logical and can be supported by argument or evidence. Interviewers do not look for applicants to agree with them – unless their argument in a discussion is undeniable, of course; they seek debate; it is in this that they see applicants thinking for themselves, and that is where potential for future development is most visible.

Unsuccessful applications

Every year c.10,000 unsuccessful applicants to Oxford and Cambridge, for instance, go on to achieve grades AAA or better at A level. Oxbridge could happily take many more of these were the places available; the 'unsuccessful' are, by and large, excellent students; it's just that there are lots of other excellent students out there, and so some of the excellent have to be disappointed. This is no comment on them; it is a comment on the scale of the competition. Applicants to any very selective university must, therefore, be both realistic and philosophical about their prospects. The key thing is that they win a place at a really good university to read a subject in which they are truly interested. Universities will usually provide feedback to unsuccessful applicants on request, though this is not always as informative as applicants would like. Re-applications to the most sought-after courses are sometimes successful.

Richard Partington, Senior Tutor, Churchill College Cambridge

Part Two: A-Z of university subjects

Accountancy
(also banking, finance and insurance)

Essential A levels None.
Useful A levels Possibly maths and economics.

Chance of being interviewed Most applicants are offered places on the basis what is in UCAS Apply, but there is a chance you may be interviewed.

What you need to know

- An accountancy course will not train you to become a professional in the field: you will still have to complete professional qualifications after your degree. However, you will normally be exempted from some parts of the professional course.
- You should try to get some work experience in a finance-related industry. Identify what you have learned from the experience in order to discuss it in an interview.
- Make sure you have some understanding of what the industries of accountancy, finance, insurance and banking involve and be clear about why you want to work in them. For example, accountancy is concerned with the management of money, but a degree may not just lead to a job as a chartered accountant. Graduates may go into high finance, or general management, or become entrepreneurs.
- Find out as much as you can from the websites of the industries' professional bodies listed here.

Accountancy
The Institute of Chartered Accountants in England and Wales: www.icaew.co.uk
The Association of Chartered Certified Accountants: www.accaglobal.com
The Chartered Institute of Management Accountants: www.cimaglobal.com
The Chartered Institute of Public Finance and Accountancy: www.cipfa.org.uk
Retail banking
IFS School of Finance: ifslearning.ac.uk
Building Societies Association: www.bsa.org.uk
Investment and Corporate Banking
London Investment Banking Association: www.liba.org.uk
Insurance
The Chartered Insurance Institute: www.cii.co.uk
Financial Services Skills Council: www.fssc.org.uk

Sample interview questions

- What is the difference between a certified and a management accountant?
- What is accountancy?

- Why does a career in accountancy/banking/insurance interest you?
- Why do you want to do this degree rather than a business studies degree?
- If you can become an accountant after any degree, why do you want to specialize now?

- What is auditing? What is management consultancy?
- Who is to blame for the credit crunch?
- What is a sub-prime mortgage?

- Have you looked at any of the websites of the professional bodies? What did you find out?
- What did the accountancy firm you visited on your work experience do? Who were its clients?

Actuarial science/studies

Essential A levels Maths.
Useful A levels Further maths and economics.

Chance of being interviewed Many applicants will be offered places on the basis of what is in UCAS Apply, but some applicants are interviewed.

What you need to know

- Actuaries calculate insurance and pension risks using statistical techniques.
- You need to be very good at maths and very interested in financial issues.
- You will need to stick at it: you will have more years of professional training after graduation.
- Try to meet an actuary and talk to them about what the job involves.
- Visit www.actuaries.org.uk.

Sample interview questions

- What are the tasks of an actuary?
- Why do you want be an actuary?

- What are your favourite areas of maths and why?
- What did you learn from your work experience with the pensions company?

- What are the three organisations that are responsible for regulating the UK financial system?
- How could an ageing population affect the pensions industry?
- What are the insurance implications of higher levels of car crime in some inner-city areas?
- From what you have studied in A level maths, can you think of a possible statistical method to help us calculate car insurance premiums?

Agriculture

What you need to know

- You should have work experience in farming.
- You must be up to date with current political and economic issues in farming.
- Visit www.ukagriculture.com.
- Lantra is the Sector Skills Council for the environmental and land-based sector, representing 17 industries across the whole of the United Kingdom including: land management and production; animal health and welfare; environmental industries. Visit www.lantra.co.uk.
- Look at the sample interview questions under: 'Biology', 'Business studies' and 'Veterinary science'.

American studies

Essential A levels Requirements vary, but English and History are often asked for.
Useful A levels Politics.

Chance of being interviewed Interviews are more common than for other humanities degrees. This is because people often have misconceptions about the course they are applying for.

What you need to know

- If you want to study some literature, some history and some politics, and get to study at a foreign university, then this could be the course for you.
- Courses vary. Some offer the chance to study film, music or visual arts. Others are more like a traditional English or history degree. Make sure you know which you are applying for.
- Expect questions on American literature that you have read (questions will mostly be based on what you have put in your personal statement).
- Expect questions on American history.

- If there is an American election pending, or if there has just been one, it is a good idea to demonstrate analytical reading of relevant press coverage.
- Visit www.americansc.org.uk.

Sample interview questions

- Do you have any personal or family reasons for wanting to do American studies?
- Do you think American culture is overwhelming British culture?
- What do you think are the social problems facing Britain today?

- What American literature have you read away from your set texts?
- Will J D Salinger be remembered in 200 years time? Why or why not? What about Jack Kerouac?
- What was the context in which John Steinbeck wrote *The Grapes of Wrath*?

- What current American political issues interest you?
- What are the differences between the Democrats and Republicans?

- What do you hope to gain from your time at an American university?
- Do you know which American and Canadian universities are linked with our university?

- What can Barack Obama really change?
- Do you think the UK will ever have a black prime minister?
- What do you know about the sub-prime crisis?
- What are the similarities and differences between the US involvement in Vietnam and Iraq?

Anatomy

See sample interview questions under: 'Biology', 'Medicine' and 'Physiology".

Animal sciences

What you need to know

- Look at the sample interview questions under: 'Biology' and 'Veterinary science'.
- For specialist courses, such as equine science and animal welfare management, relevant work experience or voluntary work will be vital.
- Lantra is the Sector Skills Council for the environmental and land-based sector, representing 17 industries across the whole of the United Kingdom including: land management and production; animal health and welfare; environmental industries. Visit www.lantra.co.uk.

Anthropology

Essential A levels None.
Useful A levels For a small number of courses, sociology or a science A level such as biology is helpful.

Chance of being interviewed Many applicants will be offered places on the basis of what is in UCAS Apply, but some courses do still interview.

What you need to know

- Be very clear in your own mind that you understand what anthropology is. It is the study of human behaviour, beliefs, institutions and the various societies in which people live.
- Think about whether you are interested in the social or biological aspects of anthropology, or both.
- Interviews will tend to focus on comments made in your personal statement.
- Interviewers are looking for evidence of interest (books you have read, museums you have visited, overseas visits). If you have travelled abroad, can you compare other societies with your own?
- Check if the course will involve field work and whether you will be funded to do this.

Sample interview questions

- What made you decide to apply for anthropology?
- Have any of your A level subjects influenced your interest and why?

- What do you read when you are not studying?

- What tensions do you think the Inuit deal with?
- Do all societies have heroes?
- Why do we need laws?
- How has life changed for men in the last fifty years?
- Why do some societies try to impose their values and beliefs on to others?
- Explain the national grief during Princess Diana's funeral.
- Tell me about water irrigation in North Africa.
- What are the primary societies studied by anthropologists?
- What impact has globalization had on anthropological studies?
- If an alien came to earth how would you explain the differences between people and animals?
- Can you truly gain an insight into a civilization through the lives of normal people?
- Do normal people in different societies really live such different lives from one another.
- Is the evolution of visual culture linked to Darwin's theory of evolution?
- Does visual culture have anything to do with survival of the fittest?
- How does secularism affect different parts of the world?

- Have humans stopped evolving?

Students' comments

- 'I was surprised that I wasn't asked at all why I wanted to study anthropology. I also didn't talk about much of what was in my statement or my essay, and they seemed not to want me to refer to ideas in the books I had read, even specifically asking me not to at one point.

- 'I felt they were deliberately testing me on things I didn't know, so it is difficult to tell if I gave them good enough answers.'

- 'I was given an object and asked to interpret what it might indicate about a society.'

Archaeology

Essential A levels None.

Chance of being interviewed While many courses will make you an offer on the basis of what is in UCAS Apply, a significant minority will interview.

What you need to know

- Really do try and get some experience of excavations and digs (visit www.britarch.ac.uk).
- Do as much introductory reading about archaeology as you can.
- Think about how the study of archaeology helps us to understand history.
- If the course involves overseas trips, will financial help be available?

Sample interview questions

- Why do you want to do a course in archaeology?
- Which do you prefer: archaeology or prehistory?

- Do people learn from history?
- Why should money be spent on archaeology when medicine needs so much?
- Why should taxpayers spend several thousand pounds a year for you to study archaeology?
- Who cares if evidence of an ancient basket-weaving tribe is found in southern Italy?

- How can we date artefacts? Are there any other methods besides radiocarbon dating?
- What are the arguments for and against keeping the Parthenon marbles (Elgin marbles) at the British Museum?

- What countries have you travelled to? What did you learn from your experiences?
- Have you visited any archaeological sites? Which ones?
- If you were given £1million to excavate an archaeological site would you focus on the relics of the elite or the commoners?

Student's comment

- 'There were (luckily) few questions about archaeology itself and nothing on ancient history. The interviewer did, however, give me an address to contact when I said I wanted to go on a dig in my year off.'

Architecture

Essential A levels For a small number of degree courses art is required. Some universities ask for an arts/science mix. *NB A portfolio of drawings and ideas is often essential.*
Useful A levels Art, maths and physics.

Chance of being interviewed Most courses will interview and inspect portfolios but the number that are doing this is declining.

What you need to know

- It is essential to show an interest in the history of architecture (for example classical Greek and Roman, Gothic, organic and international styles) and the work and influence of architects such as Vitruvius, William of Sens, Frank Lloyd Wright and Le Corbusier. There are many books on this but a good starting point is *The Story of Architecture* by Jonathan Glancey.
- You must have a portfolio of drawings including your own ideas for buildings and drawings of existing buildings. Other artwork could be included as an addition.
- You must be able to talk about your ideas. Think about the three elements of design: the look, the cost and the making.
- You will need to have confirmed your commitment to a career in architecture through work experience.
- Remember that architecture is a multi-disciplinary profession requiring a combination of artistic, technological and sociological expertise. The challenge of architecture is to produce, within a given budget, an aesthetically pleasing design which will stand up to wear and tear and is the kind of building people would like to live or work in.
- Visit the website of the Royal Institute of British Architects: www.architecture.com.
- Visit www.greatbuildings.com.

Sample interview questions

- Why do you want to study architecture? How long have you wanted to be an architect?
- Architecture is an underpaid and overworked profession, so why do you want to go into it?
- Schools of architecture each have their own strengths and specialities. Why did you choose to apply to study architecture at this particular university?

- Are there any buildings that have particularly influenced you?
- Do you have a favourite contemporary architect? Who is it and why?
- Describe a building that you like, of any style or period.

- What do you know about the architectural styles of the 18th and 19th centuries, i.e. neoclassicism, the Gothic revival and romantic architecture?
- Describe the front of St Paul's Cathedral in London.

- Have you read any books about architecture? Which ones?
- How have you tried to broaden your knowledge and understanding of architecture?
- Do you think your A levels are relevant to studying architecture?

- Do you think that the redevelopment of the Docklands area in London has been successful?
- How do you think office blocks should be designed?
- Do you have anything against buildings showing their structures outwardly?
- Finland has a much higher percentage of women architects than Britain. Why do you think that is?

- Why are you interested in landscape architecture?
- Do you think community landscaping is important and why?

Students' comments

- 'I was asked to solve some 3D problems on a piece of paper, which I couldn't do, but the interviewer refused to let me give up until I'd at least got close. As a result I spent about ten to fifteen minutes on two problems.'

- 'While I showed the interviewer my portfolio he maintained a perfectly blank expression and made no comments.'

- 'I was asked very specific questions about periods of architectural history, which is hard with a subject like architecture because you don't study it at school. These questions only show how well you've been drilled for the interview, not whether you will be a creative and good architecture student.'

- 'I was told in a letter about the interview to be prepared to answer questions on modern architecture, construction and the building industry, but none was asked. However, the interviewer was very interested in all the artwork in my portfolio.'

- 'Just before my interview I was asked to read an article on the Architecture of Schools, which I was then questioned on.'

Art and design

Essential A levels Art or design A level/AGCE/Diploma. These will allow you to build up the portfolio you need to get on to an art foundation course. *NB Most entrants to art and design degrees will have done a one-year art foundation course after their A levels. Some AGCE/Diploma art and design students gain entry to higher education courses without doing a foundation course.*

What you need to know

Mostly, artistic sixth-form students take art A level, which is the study of painting, drawing and sculpture. Yet most university students in this field study design subjects such as graphic design, fashion design, product design and interior design. An art foundation course acts as a bridge between A levels and design degrees.

The normal attributes of an art foundation course are as follows.
- It is one year long, full time.
- Fees are not normally charged if you take the course while you are still eighteen years old.
- In the first term you will try out all the major areas of design – graphic, fashion, product, interior and others depending on the course.
- In the second term you will try to decide which area of art and design you would like to specialize in. You will begin to concentrate on this area so that you have a specialist portfolio ready for the degree/Foundation Degree or HND course you wish to apply for.
- You will be expected to work hard on your drawing skills throughout the course.
- It is a very intense year and it is not an easy option. By the time you have completed the course you should know whether art and design is for you or not. If you feel that you do not want to do a degree in art or design then you can apply for other degrees on the strength of the A levels that you have.
- It is very common for students to start an art foundation course thinking that they want to do a certain sort of design (for example, fashion) and then, once they have tried out everything else, to decide to do something different (for example, illustration).
- Most art and design degrees and HND courses make the successful completion of an art foundation course an entry requirement.

- Visit the websites of the National Society for Education in Art and Design (www.nsead.org), the Design Council (www.designcouncil.org.uk) and the Creative and Cultural Skills Council (www.ccsills.org.uk).

Sample interview questions

- How did you design and make some of the pieces in your portfolio? Why did you choose a particular style?
- Which is your favourite piece of work from your portfolio?
- What do you think is good about your drawing?
- What motivates and inspires you?
- Which aspects of the art foundation course do you particularly wish to pursue?
- What kind of career are you considering after completing your art foundation course?

- What examples of industrial design inspire you?
- What types of graphic design interest you? Give me examples. Who do you think has influenced this designer?
- Choose a piece in your portfolio? Why have you selected it?
- Is fine art design?
- Which fashion designers have you looked at? What is different about their work?
- How many sections will you need to make this garment?

- Who are your favourite artists?

Students' comments

- 'There were no questions, just a review of my portfolio. It is really important to make sure all your good work is in your portfolio, and to include a wide range of work.'

- 'It wasn't really like an interview. We had a group talk about the textile design course and then we were shown round the department. Then they saw us individually but there were no questions. They just told us what they thought of our portfolios.'

- 'I was left feeling in great doubt about the quality of my work.'

- 'One thing that I was quite pleased about was that the interviewer told me what was good and bad about my work. He told me how I could improve my style in my year off.'

Astronomy

What you need to know

- Look at the sample interview questions under: 'Physics' and 'Maths'.
- Wider reading and visits to observatories will be important.

Biochemistry

Essential A levels Always chemistry. Some degrees will say you must have biology as well. Others will ask for chemistry plus one of maths, physics or biology. Doing chemistry, biology and maths or physics will keep all biochemistry courses open to you.

What you need to know

- Biochemistry is the study of biology at a molecular level.
- Look at the sample questions under: 'Biology', 'Chemistry', 'Natural sciences' and 'Physiology'.
- Visit the website of the Biochemical Society: www.biochemistry.org.
- Cogent is the Sector Skills Council for the chemicals and pharmaceuticals, oil and gas, petroleum and polymer industries. Visit www.cogent-ssc.org.

Sample interview questions

- How do enzymes work?
- How do mutations effect bonding and folding amino acids?
- Explain how gel electrophoresis works.
- What bonding takes place within individual DNA nucleotide bases?

Biology

Essential A levels Biology and chemistry.
Useful A levels Maths or physics.

Chance of being interviewed Most courses will make you an offer on the basis of what is in UCAS Apply but a significant minority of courses still interview.

What you need to know

- You need to be fascinated by the living world and have examples to prove this that you can talk about in the interview.
- Questions will cover topics that you have already studied for your biology A level.
- Degree courses can involve much independent research, so examples of your interest in biology outside of school will be useful.
- If you are applying for a more specialist course (for example, botany) can you explain why?
- Look at the sample questions under 'Physiology'.
- Visit the website: www.iob.org.

Sample interview questions

- Why do you enjoy biology and which aspects of the subject do you like most?
- Why didn't you apply to study medicine, rather than anatomy and developmental biology?
- You want to study cell biology, so why are you *not* taking chemistry A level?
- What kind of career are you interested in pursuing after your degree?
- Tell us about the fieldwork you have done for your biology and geography A levels.

- Tell us about one main theory of cell biology.
- Why do you think free-living chloroplasts 'decided' to form into membrane-bound cells?
- How can you show the differences between a free-living chloroplast and one from a cell?
- Describe the structure of an amino acid. What are the properties of the amino and carboxyl groups? Tell us about the formation of peptide bonds.
- What do you know about protein folding?
- Describe the structure of DNA.
- Tell us about the sequencing of the human genome. What else do you know about the human genome project?
- What features make fungi different?

- In the study of human sciences, how can you make a connection between economics and biology?
- Can theories in economics and biology fully mix in a society?
- How is maths used in biology? Is it important?
- Why are you interested in epidemiology?

- What articles have you read in the *New Scientist*?
- What do you think about human cloning and other biology-related issues currently in the news?
- What do you think about animal/human dissection?
- How would you go about curing cancer?
- What nutritional problems are caused by famine?

- What are the issues when a society relies on one main type of foodstuff?
- What are the benefits of genetically modified foods? Are there disadvantages?
- What do you think is the value of gardening programmes?
- Tell us what you know about acid rain.
- What is the difference between nature studies and ecology?
- Why do you want to study zoology?
- How do you investigate animal behaviour experimentally?
- Look at this object [an elephant's tooth]. Guess what it is.

Students' comments

- 'The two interviewers began by quizzing me on A level biology concepts by asking me straightforward questions and getting me to draw things on the blackboard. Then they threw in some difficult, advanced chemistry and expected me to take the discussion to a biochemistry degree level. I was not able to do this well at all and I had to say "I don't know" many times. Much of the interview was spent with them explaining principles of biochemistry to me, which I still found very difficult to follow.'

- 'I was shown round the whole department and asked if I had seen such equipment before. Everything was explained to me, but if I had known beforehand what equipment I would be shown it would have helped.'

- 'We were shown a lot of the labs, but it was very much a case of "look but don't touch". A lot of the equipment was very expensive.'

- 'When he asked me about acid rain I couldn't answer sufficiently and so I asked him to explain to me so that I learnt something. He seemed pleased by the fact that I wanted to learn.'

Biotechnology

See sample interview questions under: 'Biology', 'Chemistry', 'Natural sciences' and 'Physiology'.

Botany

See sample interview questions under: 'Biology', 'Chemistry', 'Natural sciences' and 'Physiology'.

Building

What you need to know

- You should have a clear idea about why you want to enter this career field and evidence to support this (for example, work experience or talks with building professionals).
- Look at the sample interview questions under: 'Architecture', 'Engineering' and 'Surveying'.
- Visit the websites www.ciob.org.uk and www.constructionskills.net.

Sample interview questions

- Tell me about a construction project in your local area?
- How do you know that you can lead a team?
- What are some of the different jobs that are in the building industry?
- Are you prepared to travel with your work?

Business studies and management

Essential A levels None.
Useful A levels Possibly maths and economics.

Chance of being interviewed Most courses will make offers on the basis of what is in UCAS Apply.

What you need to know

- The subjects that are always studied for these degrees are: economics; human resources; marketing; accounting; finance; and, usually, quantitative methods (statistics) and IT. Try to get across to an interviewer that you can cope with a wide range of subjects.
- Do not be concerned about the plethora of different course names. Business studies, business and management, business management, management studies, business administration, commerce and so on – it's all essentially the same thing.
- Some courses allow you to specialize in a particular field (for example, marketing) by the end of the course. Others stay general to the end.
- Think about your personal qualities and what you have learned from any work experience or part-time work you have done. Any evidence of working in a team would be particularly useful.
- Visit Chartered Management Institute: www.managers.org.uk.

- Other websites to visit include: the Financial Services Skills Council www.fssc.org.uk.
- People 1ˢᵗ, the Sector Skills Council for the hospitality, leisure, travel and tourism industries. People 1ˢᵗ covers: contract food service providers, events, gambling, holiday parks, hospitality services, hostels, hotels, membership clubs, pubs, bars and nightclubs, restaurants, self catering accommodation, tourist services, travel services and visitor attractions. www.people1st.co.uk.
- Skillsmart, the sector skills council for the retail sector www.skillsmartretail.com
- SkillsActive is the Sector Skills Council for the active leisure and learning industry embracing sport and fitness, outdoors and adventure, playwork, camping and caravanning. www.skillsactive.com

Sample interview questions

- Why do you want to study business when your A levels are not directly linked to it?
- What specific areas of business are you interested in and why?

- Define marketing.
- What types of marketing are there?
- Could you market a product or service you do not believe in?
- What is direct marketing?
- Do you know what below-the-line marketing is?
- What do you think will be the most important industries in Britain in the next decade and after?
- What do you think about Sunday trading?
- What is the difference between a clearing bank and an investment bank?
- How can businesses make money out of leisure time?
- Is the customer always right?

- What qualities should a manager have?
- What skills are needed in hospitality management?
- What role does teamwork play in hospitality management?
- Can you think of examples of good and bad restaurant management?

- Tell us about any work experience you have had.
- Have you done any part-time work? If so, how would you improve the company you worked for?

- Do you think large supermarkets are a good or bad thing for customers?
- Why are some people unhappy in their jobs even when they are paid well?

Students' comments

- 'Apart from the actual interview there was also a group discussion session, where they monitored our behaviour and reactions within a group.'

- 'We were placed in groups of five and each group was assigned a first-year student to be with us for the day. In the afternoon my group had to go into a room and discuss a particular issue, while the student, a lecturer and a retailer quietly listened and observed us.'

Chemistry

See sample interview questions under 'Natural sciences'.

Essential A levels Chemistry and usually maths or physics. Some courses ask for chemistry, maths and physics, while some prefer chemistry, maths and biology.

Chance of being interviewed Most universities will make offers based on the content of the UCAS Apply, but a significant minority still interview.

What you need to know

- You will probably be asked questions on what you have studied at A level.
- Any extra reading of scientific journals and knowledge about science issues in the news would go down well with interviewers.
- Try to find out about the practical applications of chemistry, such as food science or the pharmaceutical industry.
- Cogent is the Sector Skills Council for the chemicals and pharmaceuticals, oil and gas, petroleum and polymer industries. Visit www.cogent-ssc.org.
- Visit www.rsc.org.

Sample interview questions

- Why do you want to study chemistry?
- What is your favourite topic in chemistry? Why do you like it?
- What kind of career are you considering after finishing your chemistry degree?

- Why is sodium chloride soluble in water and barium sulphate insoluble?
- What do you get if you react benzene with chlorine?
- How do you know that carbon forms a tetrahedral structure?
- What reactions do halogenoalkanes undergo and why?
- Draw some half-cells and discuss redox equilibria.
- What is special about transition metal compounds?
- Why is copper sulphate blue?
- How can you tell that sodium chloride is bonded ionically?

- What is a covalent bond?
- What is the most recent chemistry experiment you have carried out? Describe it.

- Compare bonding in N_2 to P_4.
- Compare bonding in NaCl (common salt) to diamond.
- What are your views on animal testing?
- Compare Flourine's compounds to Caesium's compounds.
- Draw propanone. Show its reactions with H^+/OH^-
- Compare acid chlorides and amides.
- Use a phase diagram to understand how changing conditions induce state changes in water.
- Discuss why water's phase diagram differs from other liquids.
- What are the mechanisms for nucleophilic substitution?
- What is the measure of acid strength?
- How many molecules are there in this glass of water?
- NaCl has a cubic structure with a spacing of 0.24nm between each ion. Use this to calculate an estimate for its density.
- Assuming that carbon is 99% ^{12}C and hydrogen is 99.99% ^1H, what is the probability that a molecule of C_nH_{2n+2} has exactly K ^{12}C atoms and L ^1H atoms?
- What is entropy?
- If you didn't have an indicator, how can you test the pH and equivalence point of a titration?
- What nitrogen oxides do you know? Explain the structure of nitrogen monoxide and explain the significance of its unpaired electron.
- What is the importance of chirality in Chemistry?

Students' comments

- 'I was asked lots of A level chemistry questions, which I hadn't expected at all.'

- 'Both my interviews were subject based. One was organic and the other physical and inorganic. I was asked to discuss a topic of my choice and they developed it from there. The questions asked were quite demanding because they wanted you to answer in depth. They didn't want plain facts – they wanted you to think why things happen, apply your existing knowledge and predict reactions you hadn't come across before.'

Classics/classical studies

Essential A levels For some classics courses, Latin or ancient Greek are required (you may have to translate some text at interview).
Useful A levels Classical civilization, English literature and history.

Chance of being interviewed You should presume that you will get some interviews.

What you need to know

- For a classics degree, you will normally be required to have an A level in Latin or ancient Greek. For classical studies or classical civilization, however, most A levels would be considered.
- If not ancient Greek or Latin, some flair for languages will definitely help with this course.
- The course covers literature, drama, history, politics and philosophy. It is suitable for students who enjoy reading books and thinking about the ideas behind them.
- Try to visit museums with relevant collections and ancient sites (in Rome or Greece if possible!).
- Interview questions will often relate to what you have studied already, especially if you have studied ancient Greek, Latin or classical civilization. Most other questioning will tend to refer to what you have put in your personal statement.
- If the course involves Latin or Greek literature you may be given a passage and some questions to read through just before the interview.
- If you are being interviewed for a course including classical archaeology and ancient history you may be asked to examine and discuss an ancient artefact such as a coin or pot.
- Visit www.classicspage.com.

Sample interview questions

- History is a large part of a classics degree, so why aren't you studying it at A level?
- Why are you interested in classical archaeology?

- What do you think are the differences (if any) between Roman and Greek drama?
- What are the similarities between Homer and Virgil?
- What have you learnt from the dialogues of Plato?
- Is Epicurus misunderstood?
- How has Greek tragedy influenced modern literature? Give me some examples.
- If, as you say, Aristotle has influenced empirical philosophers, in what ways has this occurred?
- How is the human body represented in classical art?

Student's comment

- 'I was given a test where I had to translate a made-up language.'

Community and youth studies

What you need to know

- Look at the sample interview questions under: 'Education', 'Professions allied to medicine', 'Sociology' and 'Social work'.
- Relevant experience or voluntary work will be important.
- Visit the website for the sector skills council for care and development: www.skillsforcareanddevelopment.org.uk.
- Visit www.csv.org.uk.

Computer courses

Essential A levels Some courses require maths. A very small number of courses like further maths.
Useful A levels Maths, physics, philosophy and ICT.

Chance of being interviewed You should presume that you will get some interviews.

What you need to know

- Computing degrees vary in their content. Make sure you know exactly what you have applied for as there is a wide range of courses on offer. Some traditional computing courses will involve you in a high level of intellectual questioning while some of the newer courses such as Digital Media will ask you questions to establish that you understand what you are applying for.
- Some courses will be very concerned about your maths ability. For others this will be less of an issue. Some courses may be interested in your design ideas.
- Try to think about all the experience you have had with computers and programming, inside and outside of school. Also, think about any work experience that may have involved computer systems. What did you learn from this? Did you have any ideas for improvement?
- Visit www.bcs.org.uk and www.e-skills.com.

Sample interview questions

- What interests you about computer science? How did you become interested in computers?
- What experience have you had of working with computers?
- What did you do for your A level computer science project?

- Why haven't you done computer science up to now? How do you know you will like it?
- What do you see yourself doing ten years from now? Will it involve computers?

- How would you find the smallest number in a list?
- How many zeros are there in 25! (i.e. factorial twenty-five)?
- How many zeros are there in 1000! (i.e. factorial one thousand)?
- Look at this set of data [provided by interviewer]. What is the minimal spanning tree?
- Using Turbo Pascal, draw a circle without using the circle command.
- Suggest a method of listing prime numbers to 1000.
- Can machines make their own decisions?
- What is in a computer?

Here are some questions from the Oxford University Computer Lab, Copyright © 2004-8 J.M. Spivey.

- *Tidy boxes.* You are given 10 boxes, each large enough to contain exactly 10 wooden building blocks, and a total of 100 blocks in 10 different colours. There may not be the same number in each colour, so you may not be able to pack the blocks into the boxes in such a way that each box contains only one colour of block. Show that it is possible to do it so that each box contains at most two different colours.
- *Searching for the maximum.* The real-valued function $f(x)$, defined for $0 \leq x \leq 1$, has a single maximum at $x = m$. If $0 \leq u < v \leq m$ then $f(u) < f(v)$, and if $m \leq u < v \leq 1$ then $f(u) > f(v)$. You are told nothing else about f, but you may ask for the value of $f(x)$ for any values of x you choose. How would you find the approximate value of m? How accurately could you find m if you could choose only 10 values of x for which to evaluate $f(x)$?
- *Death by chocolate.* You are locked in a room with your worst enemy. On a table in the centre of the room is a bar of chocolate, divided into squares in the usual way. One square of the chocolate is painted with a bright green paint that contains a deadly nerve poison. You and your enemy take it in turns to break off one or more squares from the remaining chocolate (along a straight line) and eat them. Whoever is left with the green square must eat it and die in agony. You may look at the bar of chocolate and then decide whether to go first or second. Describe your strategy.
- *Monkey beans.* An urn contains 23 white beans and 34 black beans. A monkey takes out two beans; if they are the same, he puts a black bean into the urn, and if they are different, he puts in a white bean from a large heap he has next to him. The monkey repeats this procedure until there is only one bean left. What colour is it?
- *Lily-pad lunacy.* Eleven lily pads are numbered from 0 to 10. A frog starts on pad 0 and wants to get to pad 10. At each jump, the frog can move forward by one or two pads, so there are many ways it can get to pad 10. For example, it can make 10 jumps of one pad, 1111111111, or five jumps of two pads, 22222, or go 221212 or 221122, and so on. We'll call each of these ways different, even if the frog takes the same jumps in a different order. How many different ways are there of getting from 0 to 10?
- *Missing numbers.* Imagine you are given a list of slightly less than 1,000,000

numbers, all different, and each between 0 and 999,999 inclusive. How could you find (in a reasonable time) a number between 0 and 999,999 that is not on the list?

- *Scribble.* The game of Scribble is played with an inexhaustible supply of tiles, and consists of forming `words' according to certain rules. Since each tile bears one of the letters **P**, **Q**, or **R**, these are not words that will be found in an ordinary dictionary. The game begins with the word **PQ** on the board; each move consists of applying one of the following rules:
  If the word on the board is **P**x, for some shorter word x, you may change it to **P**xx. For example, if the word is **PQRRQ** then you may change it to **PQRRQQRRQ**.
  If the word on the board is x**QQQ**y, for some shorter words x and y, then you may change it to x**R**y, replacing the sequence **QQQ** with a single **R**.
  If the word on the board is x**RR**y, for some shorter words x and y, then you may change it to xy, deleting the sequence **RR** entirely.
  (i) For each of the following words, say whether you can make it or not by following the rules of the game: **QPR**, **PQQ**, **PQR**, **PR**. (ii) Given any word, how can you decide whether it can be made or not?

  Some general hints:
- If the problem contains specific numbers (like 10, 100, 23, 34), does it become easier if we replace those numbers with smaller ones, or even by 0 or 1 or 2? If there are no specific numbers, can you solve the problem in small examples, such as a 2 x 1 bar of chocolate?
- Are there other simplifying assumptions that you can try? What if the bar of chocolate consists of just one row of squares? What if the green square is in one corner?
- Is there a way of reducing the problem as given to a smaller one? Is there a way of filling the first box of blocks that eliminates a colour, leaving us with 9 boxes and 9 colours?
- Some of these problems have definitive answers, other do not – or not answers that can be reached during a half-hour conversation, anyway. Most of them can be solved in several stages, beginning with easy cases and getting more general; some problems can be generalised beyond what is asked in the question.

Students' comments

- 'After a preliminary conversation and questioning, I was asked to solve some problems on paper. As soon as each problem was on paper they expected the solution – impatience was in the air, as was an unforgiving demand for accuracy. I'm afraid I cracked under the pressure. Applicants should be aware that the nature of pressure changes very much when one has to write, rather than talk.'

- 'A lot of the interview seemed to be based on the question, "Why did you apply for this course?" It would seem the stock response is, "Because I like computers." So a better answer to this question would probably be about why computers are important.'

Criminology

See sample interview questions under: 'Sociology', 'Law' and 'Psychology'

Dance

What you need to know

- Prepare well for auditions and take account of the differing procedures at the various schools of dance that you have applied to.
- Make sure you know whether or not the courses you are applying for will train you as a professional dancer.
- Look at the sample interview questions under: 'Drama and theatre studies'.
- Visit www.cdet.org.uk.

Dentistry

Essential A levels Chemistry and biology would be acceptable for most courses, but a few still prefer chemistry, biology and maths or physics.

Chance of being interviewed Expect to be interviewed by all of your choices.

What you need to know

- You will need to be able to explain fully why you want be become a dentist and provide evidence to back up your claims.
- Interviewers will be interested in any work experience you have done in dentistry. Can you explain what you learnt from it?
- Show your interest by being aware of some current issues or difficulties facing dentists. Is there one that you could talk about in more depth?
- Interviewers will want to know that you have a high level of manual dexterity. Try to think of things you have done that *prove* your manual dexterity.
- Most dental schools will require you to take the UKCAT: www.ukcat.ac.uk.
- Visit the websites of the British Dental Association (www.bda.org) and the General Dental Council (www.gdc-uk.org).

Sample interview questions

- Why do you want to do dentistry, rather than medicine?
- How come you want to do dentistry when you are not doing biology A level?

- What would you like to do after your dentistry degree, for example: research, a BSc or general practice?

- What qualities make a good dentist? Give some examples.
- How do you know that you are manually dexterous?
- How do you help a friend if they are anxious?
- What would you *not* like about dentistry?

- What are orthodontics?
- What is cosmetic dentistry?
- What is preventative dentistry?
- Tell us what you know about tooth decay.

- Do you know of any current issues or difficulties facing dentists today? Tell us more about one particular issue.
- Where do you see dentistry going in the future?
- Do you think that a degree in dentistry is about training or education?

- What was the most important thing you learned from your work experience?
- What do you know about the General Dental Council?
- What is meant 'to be a member of a profession'?
- What are your negative qualities.

- Why do you need a CRB check and what is it?
- What is hepatitis A? B?
- Why do dentists needs immunising?
- Tell us about your work experience.
- How do you cope under pressure?
- What are controversial issues in dentistry?
- What are your hobbies?
- What are you reading?

Students' comments

- 'I came away feeling that it was an unfair interview, but in fact I was only questioned about things I had put in UCAS Apply (though in a very challenging manner). Nothing really was asked about dentistry.'

- 'It was very important to know what you had gained from your work experience – sort of, "What is life like beside the dentist's chair?"!'

Development studies

See sample interview questions under: 'Economics', 'Geography', 'Politics', 'Sociology' and 'Anthropology'

Dietetics

See 'Professions Allied to Medicine'

Drama and theatre studies

Essential A levels Some courses require English literature. A few courses specify English and theatre studies.
Useful A levels English literature, English literature and language and theatre studies.

Chance of being interviewed Expect to be called for an interview and audition from all of your choices.

What you need to know

- If you want to enter a career in professional acting, you will find essential information on the website of the Conference of Drama Schools (www.drama.ac.uk) and the National Council for Drama Training (www.ncdt.co.uk). You need to be clear about which courses will train you to work as a professional actor and which courses are more concerned with the criticism and analysis of the theatre.
- Check whether the drama schools you are interested in handle their own applications or work through UCAS. If you need to apply directly to the school do so well before the deadline (usually March).
- Check on the schools' individual websites whether bursaries or scholarships are available.
- If you are applying for acting courses, be clear about what you have learned from all the roles you have played so far.
- If you are applying for technical courses, think about the problems you have encountered in the productions you have been involved with and how you have dealt with those problems.
- Seek advice from teachers or tutors with recent and successful experience of helping people prepare for audition.
- For an honest idea of the industry see www.equity.org.uk.
- Each initial audition will cost around £35 to £45. There is no charge if you are called back for further auditions.
- The sector skills councils for acting are: Creative and Cultural www.ccskills.org.uk and Skillset www.skillset.org.

Sample interview questions

- Which modern playwrights do you like?
- Talk about the last play you saw.
- What books do you like to read?
- In what ways would an actor benefit from learning to dance?
- Talk about Shakespeare as a dramatist.
- Tell us about the qualities you like in an actor you admire.

- What type of dance are you interested in?
- What dance experience have you had (i.e. lessons, performances)?
- What do you hope to do as a career after this course?

- When did you get into acting? How?
- Have you seen any theatre productions recently?
- Where else are you applying?

Students' comments

- 'It was not an interview, it was an audition. I had to learn three pieces to perform, of no more than two minutes each: some Shakespeare in blank verse; a contemporary work; and something of my own choice.'

- 'As well as the interview there was a 45-minute drama practical, which included mime and speech, individual and pair work. I didn't find it too difficult.'

- 'It's essential to arrive early for your dance audition so that you have plenty of time to warm up. Some dancers arrived late and got in a panic about changing and warming up.'

- 'When it came to the actual dance audition the panel made people wearing legwarmers take them off – but they didn't ask nicely at all. Being shouted at in front of a group of people you don't know is very unnerving!'

- 'Start looking for your monologues in Year 12. Most drama schools ask to see an Elizabethan or Jacobean piece. Shakespeare tends to be a good choice but you must choose a monologue that lasts roughly two minutes. The other monologue should be from a modern play. Also, prepare a back-up monologue. Check the websites or prospectuses because some have specific requirements – some even give a list of suggested audition pieces. Give yourself at least a few months to prepare and perform your pieces in front of as many people and as many times as you can.'

Economics

Essential A levels Some courses specify maths.
Useful A levels Maths and economics.

Chance of being interviewed Most courses will make offers on the basis what is in UCAS Apply, but a small number of courses still interview all applicants.

What you need to know

- Keep abreast of economic issues that are in the news.
- If you are studying economics at A level, be prepared to talk in depth about topics you have covered.
- If you are not studying economics at A Level, be prepared to do some extra reading on some economic issues that interest you. Also, think about the A Levels you *are* taking to see if they have any cross-curricular links with economics. Be prepared to talk about these.
- It is important to show that you have a genuine interest in economics – not just an interest in working for an investment bank!
- Visit www.res.org.uk and the Financial Services Skills Council www.fssc.org.uk.

Sample interview questions

- Discuss interest rate movements and their effects on the strength of a currency, imports/exports and investment.
- Is economics a science?
- Find the elasticity of a demand function: $\log q = a + b \log p$ $q = a + bp$.
- Is the current British taxation system fair? What effect do tax thresholds have? What is meant by 'the poverty trap'?
- How is inflation caused?
- What is so bad about inflation?
- What would you do to solve a country's long-term inflation problems?
- What is the impact on the UK of the credit crunch?
- What has been the impact of the minimum wage on the economy?
- If a high minimum wage leads to unemployment, would you still support it?
- What indirect taxes would you impose?
- What do you think about the inequality of earning in society? Is it right for people of higher natural intelligence to earn more money?
- What is wrong with having a balance of payments deficit? Can't a surplus be just as bad?
- What do you think about the privatisation of public utilities and the oligopolies it creates?
- Should prisons or the army be privatised?
- What would be the advantages and disadvantages of privatising the NHS?
- What are the pros and cons of European Monetary Union?

- Discuss the European Union's agricultural policy. How does it work and who does it benefit? How has it affected countries outside the EU?
- When the countries of eastern Europe joined the European Union, what were thought to be the disadvantages?
- In terms of world trade, what are the benefits for a country of being in a trade bloc?
- What are tradeable pollution permits? Are they effective?
- What do you understand by the 'sub-prime' crisis?
- How would you distinguish between a 'recession' and a 'depression'?
- What do you understand by the term 'securitisation'?

- How important are economic models?
- What is monetarism? Who started it?
- Work out, on a whiteboard, the principle of supply and demand, starting from first principles.
- In economics, what is the multiplier?
- How did the economic policies of the early 1980s, designed to combat inflation, lead to higher unemployment?
- What caused the crisis in the Asian economies in the 1990s?
- Give an example of a positive externality.
- How has globalisation affected the economy?

- What stories have you been following lately in *The Economist*?
- Do you think that *The Economist* has a political standpoint and, if so, which one?
- Discuss any major current economic problem or issue.

- What can be done to reduce pollution in the world, particularly in developing countries?
- Compare the effects of an earthquake in San Francisco and one in a developing country.
- Should we encourage nuclear power?
- What are the problems facing agriculture in Britain?
- What economic effect would a peace settlement in the Middle East have?

Students' comments

- 'It's important to be up-to-date with current affairs and to have an opinion. You also need to know about all the relevant books, journals and newspapers and be aware of their political stances.'

- 'I was asked to choose a mathematical technique or theorem (such as induction or dimensional analysis) and explain the process. Then the interviewer asked me to apply that technique to economics. It was a very unusual interview.'

- 'Most of the interview was taken up with questions on maths and statistics which the interviewer set out for me. I had to do the equations on a board in front of him.'

Education (teacher training)

Essential A levels At least one from: <u>art</u>, <u>biology</u>, <u>chemistry</u>, design and technology, drama (theatre studies), <u>English</u>, French, <u>geography</u>, German, <u>history</u>, ICT, Italian, <u>maths</u>, <u>music</u>, <u>physical education</u>, <u>physics</u>, <u>religious studies (theology)</u>, Spanish. The subjects that are underlined are those usually best for primary teaching. Courses such as CACHE and AGCE Health and Social Care are often considered for General Primary Education degrees.

Chance of being interviewed It is a requirement that all applicants for teacher training are interviewed.

What you need to know

- At interview you are normally asked to provide a short written statement on a given topic to ascertain your standard of written English.
- You must have had some sort of work experience or observational experience in a school appropriate to the age range for which you are applying.
- You must have English, maths and science GCSE at grade C or above to teach in primary education Key stage 2/3.
- You must do more than just describe your experience. What did you learn from it? What difficulties did the teachers face? What did they enjoy about the job? What initiatives were being implemented? Did you think there was too much testing?
- Is there an academic discipline you want to specialize in? If not, why not?
- Visit www.tda.gov.uk.

Sample interview questions

- Why do you want to become a teacher?
- What is a teacher's role?
- What kind of qualities should a teacher have?
- What, in your opinion and from your own experience, makes a bad teacher?
- Tell us about a teacher you admire, and why.
- What are your own good qualities and how are they relevant to teaching?
- What is your weakest subject at school?
- What experience of children have you had? Do you have experience of working with children?
- How is your work experience relevant to teaching? What has it taught you?
- What additional skills do you have that would be of benefit to a career in teaching (e.g. drama, sports)?

- What do you think about the National Curriculum?
- What do you think about recent changes in the education system?
- Discuss an educational issue that has been in the news recently.

- How would you relate to other members of staff at school? What skills would you need?
- How would you deal with prejudices in the classroom?
- Do you think you will be able to develop good relationships with parents? How?

- Why is PE important in schools? How are the skills gained from PE important later in life?
- What is the importance of teaching history in schools? In what ways can history be taught to children?

- Why do you want to specialize in teaching the youngest age group?
- Why do you particularly want to teach children with learning difficulties?
- Why do you need a CRB check and what is it?

Students' comments

- 'It was a very well-structured day. It started with a 45-minute talk about the course. Then we had to write an essay with the title, "Who is a teacher accountable to?" They said it didn't matter so much what we wrote – they were more interested in style and accuracy. Then we were interviewed individually by a local head teacher and a lecturer from the university.'

- 'I applied to specialize in English and drama. The first part of the day was a session of practical exercises in drama techniques. Then we were put into groups of six and had to do a critical analysis of some poetry. Finally, there was a personal interview.'

- 'The practical PE assessment was very tiring and physically demanding. It included running, ball skills, gymnastics (forward and backward rolls, handstand, cartwheel) and a short dance sequence.'

- 'I applied to specialize in history and they expected me to have a lot of knowledge. I was asked to identify some historical artefacts. Then they asked me how I would explain them to children and how they could be used for further work.'

- 'I was given a poem to discuss in a group.'

- 'There was a written test. I had to choose a book that I would use to teach children, explain why I would use it and how I would use it in the classroom.'

- 'We were split into groups of four. We had to choose a topic from a set of cards (the topics included school dinners, languages and SATs). We then had to choose one of these topics and make a group presentation which was observed.'

Engineering

Essential A levels Maths and physics (chemistry for chemical engineering).
Useful A levels Further maths, design and technology.

Chance of being interviewed Many courses do still interview.

What you need to know

- Make sure you know whether the courses that you are applying for will lead to you becoming a chartered or an incorporated engineer.
- If you are applying for a general engineering degree, you will need to be able to explain why. If you are applying for a more specialist engineering degree (for example, civil engineering), again, why?
- Look at the world around you. Do you see examples of engineering that fascinate you? Why do they fascinate you? How do they look? How were they made? What elements of maths and physics were used?
- Be aware of programmes such as 'a year in industry'. Visit www.yini.org.uk.
- Visit the websites of the professional bodies listed here.

Royal Academy of Engineering: www.raeng.org.uk
Institution of Civil Engineers: www.ice.org.uk
Institution of Chemical Engineers: www.icheme.org
Institution of Engineering and Technology (Electrical and Electronic): www.theiet.org
Institute of Mechanical Engineers: www.imeche.org.uk
The Royal Aeronautical Society: www.raes.org.uk

Sample interview questions

- What do you think engineering is?
- Give a dictionary definition of engineering.
- Where does your interest in engineering stem from?
- Have you had any experience of industry? Do you know anyone who works in industry?
- Have you thought about getting sponsorship?

- Consider a car accelerating up a hill. Describe all the external forces.
- How would you calculate acceleration? Apart from $F=ma$, give another way of writing Newton's second law.
- What is charge?
- Define simple harmonic motion, giving equations.
- What do you understand by the word 'acoustics'?
- What aspect of electronics are you interested in?
- How do you see the relationship between electronics and mathematics?
- What is the difference between a civil engineer and an architect?

- What do you find interesting about the new Wembley Stadium? What forces does the arch have to deal with?

- Describe an experiment you have done in physics. Where have you used what you learnt from this experiment?
- Tell us about your GCSE technology project.
- Describe the aerodynamics and electronics you designed for your GCSE technology project.
- What work have you done on computers and what programs have you written?
- You are applying to do chemical engineering, but why didn't you consider doing physics A level?

- Tell me about a particular project you have looked at in London.

Students' comments

- 'Most of the interview revolved around differential equations when applied to taps filling buckets with water, and questions about capacitors.'

- 'In the computation interview, the interviewer asked me how many questions I would need to ask to find a specific square he had chosen on a chessboard, if he could only answer my questions with yes or no and if the board had 128 squares.'

- 'I was asked specific questions about mechanics, oscillation and magnetic fields.'

- 'Both my interviews were very technical. Most questions somehow related to physics subjects (mechanics, electricity, forces and moments, etc.).'

- 'I was the only girl there out of approximately fifteen applicants.'

English

Essential A levels English literature or English literature and language.
Useful A levels History, theology/religious studies, classical civilization, modern foreign languages, Latin and ancient Greek.

Chance of being interviewed Most courses will make offers on the basis of what is in the UCAS Apply, however a significant minority of courses do still interview.

What you need to know

- You need to be genuinely enthusiastic about poems, plays and novels, from classical civilizations to the present day.

- Reading beyond your A level syllabus is essential. You will need to talk about your favourite authors, poets and dramatists and explain why you like them.
- The sample interview questions below give you an idea of the type of questioning you will face. The texts chosen for discussion, however, will tend to be those mentioned by you on your UCAS Apply.
- Try to think about issues relating to literature in a wider context, such as the difference between studying a text in depth or reading it for pleasure, and its links with history and religion.
- For background reading look at: *Literary Theory: A Very Short Introduction* by Jonathan Culler and *Beginning Theory: An Introduction to Literary and Cultural Theory (Beginnings)* by Peter Barry.
- Most degrees are literature based so do *not* go on about creative writing and journalism!
- Poetry forms the basis or many interviews and pre-interview tests.

Sample interview questions

- Who is your favourite nineteenth- or twentieth-century novelist?
- What do you think of the character of Fanny Price in Jane Austen's *Mansfield Park*?
- In *Great Expectations* by Charles Dickens, how limiting is the use of the first-person form of narration?
- In *The Return of the Native* by Thomas Hardy, what do you think Egdon Heath represents?
- Do you think novels such as those of Jane Austen should be adapted for the screen?

- Which of Shakespeare's plays have you read, other than those you have studied at school?
- How would you define Shakespearean tragedy?
- What do you think of the ending of *King Lear*?
- How do you think the opening scene of *King Lear* influences the rest of the play?
- What does the interaction between the mad Lear and the disguised Edgar communicate and achieve?
- Is *Macbeth* Shakespeare's greatest tragedy?
- What should one feel about the character of Macbeth?
- What do you think Shakespeare suggests about the character of Macbeth in the scene in which he hallucinates and thinks he can see a dagger?
- What do you consider to be the main theme of *Othello*?
- Why does Othello shy away from talking about sex?
- Describe the sexual tension in *Much Ado About Nothing*. What does it tell us?
- What are the dramatic failures in *Hamlet*?

- Discuss Chaucer's art.
- Do you think Chaucer's *Wife of Bath's Tale* represents women well?
- How is *The Wife of Bath's Tale* relevant to today?
- Do you think the wife of Bath is a strong character?

- Choose a poem you have read and discuss its imagery, sentence structure, tone and meaning.
- Recite 'On a Grecian Urn' by Keats and then analyse it.
- Discuss some poems from *The Whitsun Weddings* by Philip Larkin.
- Analyse the poem 'Harrow-on-the-Hill' by John Betjeman.
- Was William Wordsworth patronizing towards his sister Dorothy?
- What do you think of the poetry in Ben Jonson's play *Volpone*?
- What poetry do you read outside of school and why do you enjoy it?

- What book are you reading at the moment? Are you enjoying it and, if so, why?
- Compare *Bridget Jones's Diary* by Helen Fielding to *The Secret Diary of Adrian Mole aged 13¾* by Sue Townsend.

- What is the relationship between literature and art?
- How would you approach translating a text?
- Why would a writer bother to write a play when it will inevitably be subject to interpretation from the actors and director?
- When does satire become cynicism?
- Discuss the importance of 'context' in literature.
- How is Shakespeare's approach to tragedy different from Aristotle's? Is it different at all?

- What is the importance of feminist criticism?
- Apply your criticisms of the feminist perspective to Austen's 'Pride and Prejudice.'
- Apply a Marxist perspective to a novel of your choice. Then to the same novel apply a feminist perspective.
- How much of a sociological impact can a piece of literature have?
- What do you read for fun?
- What would you consider literature?
- Is anything literature?
- Are the lyrics of Eminem literature?
- Can you apply a literary analysis to anything?
- Why study English?
- Are you not angry at the silence of women in literature?

- Define the words: metre, ballad, phrase, genre, pronoun.
- What are the issues with transferring a book to a screenplay?
- What do you know about critics? What is the importance of critics? Can you quote one?
- In this day of Xboxes and Playstations and all the mechanisms vying for our attention, what would be your argument for the importance of literature?

Students' comments

- 'Having taken a year out, I found it quite difficult to discuss Shakespeare in great detail, especially *Macbeth*, which I studied for GCSE.'

- 'The interview was based almost wholly on poetry and a good base of knowledge was imperative. It seemed almost like a verbal practical criticism. Every statement I made had to be fully supported.'

- 'Make sure you are thoroughly familiar with the work of at least two poets. It is important to be confident and the only way you will be is if you are familiar with all your texts and a base of poetry.'

- 'I was handed a lengthy poem, told to read it and asked to deliver a practical criticism. This was a bit nerve-racking but I think it is important to take your time to read and absorb the text and form your own opinions.'

- 'It is vital to know your texts well and it is worth preparing a couple of books that aren't on the syllabus for a discussion about your private reading.'

- 'I was asked to read over a poem and then discuss it with the interviewer. Then I was asked to speak for five minutes on a book of my choice (unprepared).'

- 'They are impressed if you use short memorized quotes to illustrate the points you make, especially from the poetry you study.'

- 'I would recommend knowing your personal statement and the books it mentions very thoroughly.'

- 'I was given a poem with a missing line. I then had too fill in the missing line and explain what I was trying to say.'

- 'I was given two openings from 19th century novels and I had to explain which opening I thought was most effective.'

- 'Good job I like poetry. It all seemed to be about unseen poems.'

Environmental health

What you need to know

- Environmental health officers ensure that people are protected from a wide range of hazards in the environment in its widest sense. To find out more, visit the website of the Chartered Institute of Environmental Health: www.cieh.org.
- You will need to be able to explain fully why you want be become an environmental health officer. Can you provide evidence to back up your claims?
- If you have done some work experience in environmental health, can you explain what you learnt from it?
- Be aware of some current issues or difficulties facing environmental health officers. Is there one that you could talk about in more depth?
- Try to identify anything in the subjects you have studied so far that relates to environmental health. Be prepared to expand on this.
- Think about the qualities you would need to be a good environmental health officer. Try to give examples.

European studies

See 'Languages'

Film, radio and TV studies

See 'Media and communication studies'

Finance

See sample interview questions under: 'Accountancy', 'Business studies' and 'Economics'

Geography, geology and environmental science

Geography
Essential A levels Most degrees require geography.
Useful A levels Some BSc degrees prefer one of: biology, chemistry, maths or physics.
Geology/Earth sciences
Essential A levels Usually two from: maths, physics, chemistry and biology.
Useful A levels Geography and geology.

Environmental science/studies
Essential A levels Many courses will ask for two from: biology, chemistry, maths, physics and geography or geology.

Chance of being interviewed Most courses will make offers on the basis of the UCAS Apply but a significant minority of courses do still interview.

What you need to know

- Be prepared to talk in detail about field visits you have been on.
- Make sure you are as aware as possible about your own locality. Show that you have taken in as much as possible of the world around you. Also have an awareness of world issues.
- Expect questions on the parts of the A level geography syllabus that you have covered.
- Mention any magazines that you have read or TV programmes that you have watched, but then be prepared to answer some in-depth questions on these.
- These courses contain many practical elements – they are about doing not just thinking. So try to think of examples where you have actually done and completed something, rather than just thought about it.
- You may be given a map/specimen of rock or indeed any relevant object to reflect upon and discuss.
- Visit www.geography.org.uk.

Sample interview questions

- What is the definition of geography?
- Why study geography? What do you like about it?
- Which areas of geography do you like best?
- What interests you in the field of geology?
- Why are you interested in earth sciences?

- Look at these photographs. What landforms do they show and what types of rocks form these features?
- Tell us what you know about plant succession on dunes.
- Talk about the geography of a country you know.

- What era do you think the buildings in Manchester date from?
- What is special about London as opposed to other cities in England?
- What are the environmental problems in the area that you live?
- What is waste?
- Explain the Burgess Model. What happens when the periphery can no longer support the core?

- What did you learn on your geography field trip?
- What experience of field work do you have?
- From the graph showing 40 years of carbon dioxide emissions what can you conclude?
- How can you apply the statistics you have learnt on your geography A level course?
- In what areas do you think sociology and geography overlap?
- What are the benefits and problems of a hydro-electric plant being built in a rural region in North America which is home to a native tribe?

- What are the arguments for 'trade not aid'?
- What books or articles about geography have you read lately?

Students' comments

- 'Know your subject well. Know current events. Know the reasons why you want to study geography.'

- 'I was asked a lot of questions relating to geography theory, which I was unprepared for as the letter did not indicate that the interview would be formal.'

- 'He asked me: "Do you have any questions?" So I asked: "How can the position of plate boundaries on the crust change?" This happened to be his area of research and so took up the whole interview!'

- 'There were 150 people in total and we were split into 13 groups. The group interview was with 3 to 4 people for an hour.'

History

Essential A levels Most degrees require history.
Useful A levels Economics, English literature, philosophy, politics, sociology and theology/religious studies.

Chance of being interviewed Most courses will make offers on the basis of the UCAS Apply, but a significant minority of courses will interview.

What you need to know

- You will need to put across your passion for history – with evidence to support this.
- Show that you are genuinely interested in periods of history other than those you are studying for your A level.
- Think about the links between history and the other subjects you may be studying (for example, English literature).
- Questions will mostly be based on your A level history syllabus, wider reading that you have mentioned in your personal statement and, in a few instances, work that you have sent in or sources that you have been given at interview.
- Try to think of examples where you have learned independently and not just relied on your teachers.
- Visit www.history.org.uk.

Sample interview questions

- Why is history important?
- Is history really relevant to the present? Even ancient history?
- Why do you want to study history and not science, when the world is crying out for more scientists?
- What are the differences and similarities between the sciences and history?
- How is history taught at your school?
- What is the library like at your school?
- What important books have you read?
- How do the citizens of a country influence its foreign policy?

- Did Cromwell use his religious beliefs to mask his personal ambition? Why did he execute the King?
- Free trade or fair trade?

- What area of history are you most interested in?
- What has been you favourite topic in the history you have studied?
- What are you studying in British and European history for your A level?
- What history books have you read?
- How is history taught at your school and in schools generally?
- How much does history influence literature or vice versa?

- For a history essay you have written, what books did you read on the topic? How did the opinions of the various authors differ?
- How important is the role of the individual in history? Is it dangerous to attach too much importance to individuals?
- In your study of social history, what group of people do you think has been hidden from history? What sources of evidence can we gain from this group?
- What is the importance of using first-hand evidence and documents in studying history?

- How can we tell whether historical documents are reliable? Even if they are one-sided, are they still useful?
- What do you think are your personal biases when you study history?
- What do you think of 'women's history'?
- Do you think historical novels are useful for historians?
- Can we teach objectivity in history?
- What do you think people learn from the past?

- Do you think the holocaust should only be interpreted by Jewish historians?
- Is there any comparison between Hitler attacking the Sudetenland and Boris Yeltsin attacking Chechnya?

- Why are current affairs important?
- Name a situation in current affairs in which views have changed over the past fifteen years.
- What do you think of proportional representation?
- What modern trends are the political parties in Britain setting?
- What are the similarities and differences between journalistic and scholarly history?

- What career do you want to follow after studying history?
- How does your work experience relate to history?
- Three words; choose an odd one out. there is no wrong answer: educated, population, electorate. Argue your case. Then, argue the case of another one.

Students' comments

- 'The interview was generally a discussion about history and he really let me choose the period that I wanted to talk about.'

- 'I had sent in an essay on Mussolini, and particularly about his use of propaganda. The interview was a detailed discussion of the ideas in my essay.'

- 'Many of the questions about the relevance of studying history were repeated many times in different ways – so know your arguments.'

- 'My interview was more of an oral examination on the history A level syllabus. I was not expecting this and had not begun to learn my syllabus in the depth required.'

- 'I was asked questions of a very uninteresting nature that did not stretch me or give me any chance to distinguish myself. Whenever I said anything, instead of responding and engaging with me they would let my words hang and make me sound stupid. After five minutes of this they asked me to leave despite there being a scheduled 10 minutes more of interview.'

- 'I was given some sources to look at relating to an issue I knew nothing about. I was then asked questions on these sources.'

History of art

Essential A levels None.
Useful A levels Art, English literature, history, theology/religious studies, French, German, Spanish and Italian.

Chance of being interviewed Most courses will make you an offer on the basis of what is in UCAS Apply but a significant minority of courses do still interview.

What you need to know

- If you have not studied history of art before, make sure you have visited galleries and museums. You will be expected to talk about the works of art you have seen and what you felt about them.
- Questions will mostly be based on the content of your personal statement.
- You may be presented with an image, such as a painting, and asked specific questions about it.
- Visit www.artchive.com.

Sample interview questions

- Are you familiar with the main European schools of painting?
- Who are your favourite artists?
- What is your favourite period of art?

- Analyse eight paintings.
- Look at this reproduction of a Rembrandt painting and then talk about it.

- What is the difference between studying history of art and history of design?
- What do you perceive the history of design to be?
- How do you feel about studying social history as part of a course on history of design?
- Discuss the progress made in design and technology between 1850 and 1900.

- Do you think there is a difference if you look at subject directly or as a snapshot?
- Would you agree that your vision somewhat restricts your ability to look at several things at once which in a way is what camera does?

Student's comment

- 'The first interview really revolved around my personal interests, and how do these relate to art history; then I was presented with a set of images (1950s and 1970s advertisements mainly) and was asked to comment on each and subsequently compare them, perhaps defining some form of connection between the two. The second interview was more based on a discussion on specific artworks. With relation to these pieces of art I was asked about more general notions which surfaced.'

Hospitality management

What you need to know

- These courses provided the basis for careers in hospitality, including jobs such as: hotel manager, restaurant manager, professional chef and receptionist. Find out more by visiting the websites of People 1st (www.people1st.co.uk) and the Institute of Hospitality (www.instituteofhospitality.org).
- Most courses provide training in hotel and restaurant operations, as well as teaching subjects that are very close in content to a business studies degree (but with a hospitality slant).
- Relevant work experience is important.
- Look at the sample interview questions under: 'Business studies'.

Information management

What you need to know

- The information specialist has to deal with a range of sources far beyond books and other printed material. To find out more, visit the website of CILIP, the Chartered Institute of Library and Information Professionals, www.cilip.org.uk. CILIP was formed in 2002 following the unification of the Institute of Information Scientists and the Library Association.
- Look at the sample interview questions under: 'Computer courses' and 'Media and communication studies'.

International relations

See sample interview questions under: 'History' and 'Politics'

Journalism

See sample questions under 'Media and communication studies'.

Essential A Levels None
Useful A Levels Any A Levels that teach grammar (e.g. Languages). Media related courses may help establish your interest but are not asked for.

Chance of being interviewed Expect to be interviewed by many of your choices

What you need to know

- Ensure that the course is accredited by at least one of the three industry training bodies - the National Council for the Training of Journalists (print), the Periodicals Training Council and the Broadcast Journalism Training Council (radio, TV and online).
- You need evidence of a commitment to this area of work – more important than work experience (which is however useful in giving you a taste of the working environment) is evidence of doing things under your own initiative – sixth form newsletter, contributing to an unofficial football website, making podcasts etc.
- Some courses may set you an assignment or task at the interview, usually to check your writing skills.
- Visit www.bjtc.org.uk, www.ppa.co.uk (Periodicals Training Council), www.nctj.com.

Sample interview questions

- Who is your favourite broadcast journalist?
- Here are three stories. Which one would you lead with and why?
- Is there a future for newspaper journalism when we can access information in so many different ways?
- You have to describe a football match in less than 100 words. What do you think are the essential bits of information that you must include?

Languages

European studies
Essential A levels A modern European foreign language, for example, French, German, Spanish or Italian.

French
Essential A levels French.
Useful A levels Another modern foreign language.

German
Essential A levels German.
Useful A levels Another modern foreign language.

Italian
Essential A levels Italian or another language such as French, German or Spanish. Latin also useful.

Spanish
Essential A levels Spanish (some degrees will also consider French, German or Italian).

Chance of being interviewed Many courses will make offers on the basis of the UCAS Apply, but you should presume that you will get some interviews.

What you need to know

- Be prepared for some sort of grammar, comprehension, reading or translation test at the interview. You may be asked to write and/or discuss.
- Expect questions on the A level work that you have done, visits abroad and the literature, history, politics, geography and culture of the country that you are interested in.
- Read newspapers, magazines and websites in the appropriate language.
- Often more than one tutor will interview if you are applying to study more than one language.
- Visit www.languageswork.org.uk and the website of the Institute of Linguists (www.iol.org.uk).

Sample interview questions

- Why do you want to study your chosen language as opposed to any other?
- Do you think that language and literature are completely separate and should be studied separately?
- Are you better at language or literature?
- Which would you like to focus on most at university – literature or linguistics?

- Do you think being half French and wanting to do a degree in French is a cop-out?
- Are you better at French or German? Which do you prefer?
- Do you find grammar difficult?
- What are the advantages and disadvantages of translating?
- How would you teach a language? How are French and German taught at your school?
- What do you expect it will be like to learn Spanish from scratch?
- If you want to study modern languages, why are you not doing Spanish A level?
- How does your study of maths and economics relate to your language studies?
- Read this French text aloud and then translate it into English.
- Read this passage in French and then discuss it, explaining some of the vocabulary.

- [To a candidate applying to learn Italian from scratch] Look at this poem in Italian with a translation in English. Identify the meaning of each Italian word. Now look at these very different translations of the same poem and compare them.

- Is there an element of literature in your French and German A level courses?
- Have you studied literature at all? What types of literature interest you?
- Do you feel that you will be at a disadvantage doing a literature-based degree, when you are not studying any literature-based A levels?
- What books have you studied in French? Which ones did you *not* like and why?
- Have you read any French books apart from the ones on your A level syllabus?
- Look at this poem by Baudelaire for fifteen minutes, then discuss it in the interview.
- Look at this passage in French. Is it a poem or drama? What is it about the language that makes you say it is poetic?
- What French poetry have you read?

- Have you ever been to Spain? What do you know about Spain?
- What attracts you to Spanish culture?
- Have you read any Spanish literature in translation?
- How has Spain contributed to the arts and humanities?
- What do you know about Spanish architecture?
- Why would Spanish be important in a career/in business/in Europe?
- What books have you read by a Spanish-speaking author?

- What makes an English person English?
- Why is communication important in the EU?
- What do you think of a two-speed Europe and further EU integration?
- Do you think German reunification was a good thing?
- What aspect of European affairs are you particularly interested in?

- Eskimos have 50 words for snow. Russians have no word for privacy. Does this mean they don't have privacy?
- Should prisoners be entitled to privacy?
- Should immigration be allowed?

The following questions were asked and answered in the relevant foreign language.
- Have you ever been to France? What were your impressions? What shocked you?
- Pretend you are a guide and take me on a tour of the French town where you stayed.
- What are the differences between the French and the English?
- What tensions exist between the French and the English?
- What are the differences between French and English newspapers?
- Define existentialism. Do you believe in it?
- What do you think of Paris and the Parisians?
- What do you think of the National Front in France?
- What problems are linked with Algerian immigration to France?
- Tell us about the French political scene.
- Have you been to Germany? Tell us about your visit.

- Do you prefer French or German food?
- What are you studying for your history A level?
- What do you intend to do in your year off?

Students' comments

- 'The interview was conducted partly in German, partly in French and of course in English. The more intellectually demanding questions were in the main asked in English.'

- 'I was asked to translate a passage of French prose and comment on it. In my Spanish interview I spoke about my interest in foreign films which we then discussed in detail.'

- 'Although the course is not wholly based on literature, I got the impression that it is a very important part. Even in my general interview I was asked to read a poem in English and discuss it.'

- 'The grammar test took one hour and I was given a text in English which I had to answer three questions about and translate part of. No dictionaries were allowed.'

- 'I was asked some difficult questions in French about the passage they gave me to look at, which was very wordy. I was asked a lot about my further reading of French books, but all the literature and personal questions were in English.'

- 'The woman from the Italian department asked me a few questions about the reasons I wanted to study Italian, and asked me if spoke any. The fact that I couldn't speak any Italian was not a problem at all.'

- 'I was very surprised that I was only asked one question in French, and that we spoke for about twenty minutes about the books I am reading for my English A level.'

- 'We ended with a few questions in French and I had to explain (in poor French, I feel) why I started a French debating society and whether the French are actually hypochondriacs, an issue that I said we had debated.'

- 'I had to do a written test. The first part was a text in English about British and American poetry, which I had to summarize in English. The second part was a text in French, summarized with words missing. I had to find words to fill in the gaps.'

- 'I had to read a short passage and discuss it in Italian. I was then asked questions in Italian about one of the books I had been studying.'

Law

What you need to know

- You must be interested in studying law as an intellectual discipline, not just as a means to becoming a solicitor or barrister.
- Many questions will be based on what you have put in your personal statement.
- It is important, however, to read the law sections in the broadsheet newspapers and follow legal arguments in the press.
- Visit some law courts.
- Read *Learning the Law* by Glanville Williams and *Understanding the Law* by Geoffrey Rivlin.
- Visit the websites of the General Council of the Bar of England and Wales (www.barcouncil.org.uk) and the Law Society (www.lawsociety.org.uk).
- If you will be taking the LNAT test, prepare yourself by finding out about critical thinking techniques www.lnat.ac.uk.
- Visit Skills for Justice www.skillsforjustice.com.

Sample interview questions

- Why do you want to study law? What in particular interests you in the law?
- Do you want to be a judge?
- What is the point of studying law as an intellectual discipline, as opposed to, say, literature?
- How is laws more important than politics or economics?
- How does a historian's interpretation of law differ from a lawyers?

- Did you choose your A levels with the aim of studying law?
- Why do you want to study a whole new subject rather than just carrying on with one of your A level subjects?
- How has visiting courts and parliament helped you understand anything you've read in law books?
- What law books have you read?
- Have you ever visited a court? What did you think?
- You don't seem to have any relevant work experience. Why is that?

- What recent legal cases have you heard of?
- Comment on a current legal issue that interests you.

- What are the differences between and US and UK constitutions and which is more effective from a legal perspective?
- Give me an example of how the law could manifest itself in this room.

- What would you do to reform the legal system?
- What changes would you introduce to the British constitution?
- What are your views on proportional representation?
- What do you think about employment law in relation to the sacking of pregnant women?
- What is civil disobedience? Do you know any examples of it?
- How would any loss of British sovereignty to Europe affect the judiciary?
- Do you disagree with capital punishment? Why?
- What do you think about censorship?
- How do you feel about the lack of women in the higher ranks of the law?
- What do you know about the American legal system? What problems does it have?
- Why do we need laws for acts such as murder?
- What is the difference between intention and motive?
- What are the advantages and disadvantages of the right to silence?
- Define racial hatred. Distinguish between racial, religious, ethnic and political hatred. Is one worse than any other?
- How right is it to stop a crime before it has been committed?
- Is it ever justifiable to break a promise?
- Judiciary vs. legislature – who should make decisions?
- Are there any cases when laws should be broken (for example, to defeat Nazism)?
- Should Nazi war criminals be tried for their crimes?
- Should the law intervene in moral issues? What is the link between law and morals?
- Should the state interfere in family matters?
- How are the law and politics linked?
- What is the Marxist view of law? Does it still apply today?

- Are you interested in current affairs? Tell us about a recent news story.
- What do you think about the wars in Iraq?
- Why did you decide to get involved with Friends of the Earth?
- Tell us about a current economic issue.
- What books do you read? Tell us about, for example, George Orwell's *1984* and *The Prince* by Machiavelli.
- What books are you studying for your English A level?

Students' comments

- 'They gave me a paper about the General Pinochet extradition case, with some contradictory laws relating to it. I had to interpret them and answer questions such as: "Do you think Pinochet should have been extradited?" and "Does international law take precedence over human rights?"'

- 'I was given a discussion sheet with a definition of the offence of battery on it, followed by three different situations. I had to decide whether battery had been committed in each of the situations, according to the given definition.'

- 'I was given a sheet with some statutes printed on it and I was asked to read one of them (which happened to be about theft). I was then given a particular situation to respond to, which was: "Is taking someone's car road-tax disc and returning it after it has expired classified as theft?"'

- 'I had to read a long passage (a side of typed A4 paper) and then say what was illogical about it.'

- 'The legal questions forced me to think on the spot, and we discussed issues in what seemed to me to be great depth. He was interested not so much in my answers, but my reasoning.'

- 'The questioning was designed for me to respond, though at times I felt it was too aggressive. Having said that, for a law interview it seemed fair as they were able to judge my arguing skills and the way I responded to rigorous questioning.'

- 'Many of the questions posed could be interpreted in a number of ways and there was plenty of opportunity to guide the conversation to talk about the areas of law that I knew about.'

- 'In the second interview I was given a statute on a criminal act about destroying property and I was given legal problems and asked if the defendant could be prosecuted based on that statute. Then we had a debate about whether the police should keep hold of prisoners' DNA after they've been released.'

- 'We were given a legal extract (a court case) and then given 30 minutes to read it. We were then asked questions on the case.'

Leisure and recreation management

See sample interview questions under: 'Business studies' and 'Sports studies'

Linguistics

What you need to know

- Linguistics is the scientific study of languages in general – that is, how languages work and how people use language. It can cover subjects such as: how languages developed historically; phonology (the study of sounds); grammar (as it applies to all languages); meaning; the sociological aspects of language such as dialects and accents; the biological aspects of how our brains acquire language.
- Interviewers will mostly be concerned with why you want to do the course and what steps you have taken to find out about it.

Sample interview questions

- What do you understand by the term 'linguistics'?
- Name some sounds in English which foreigners get wrong.
- Talk about some grammatical structures which differ between English and another language you know.

Marketing

See sample interview questions under: 'Business studies'

Materials science
(including biomedical materials science)

See sample interview questions under: 'Biology', 'Chemistry', 'Engineering', 'Natural sciences' and 'Physics'

Maths

Essential A levels Maths and sometimes further maths.
Useful A levels Physics and philosophy.

Chance of being interviewed You should definitely expect to be called for some interviews.

What you need to know

- The interview will be about *maths*! Any questions about your social life or outside interests will only be included to put you at your ease.
- As well as your strength in maths, you need to be enthusiastic. Show proof of your love of maths – for example, through wider reading, entering competitions, joining maths clubs.
- One book worth reading before your interview is *How to solve it* by Polya.
- Visit www.ima.org.uk.

Sample interview questions

- Define the concept of differentiation using first principles.
- Give examples of situations where differentiation is *not* possible.
- How would you show that integration is the opposite of differentiation?
- How would you explain integration and differentiation to a sixth-former?
- Differentiate x^2 and sin x from first principles.
- Integrate $\int x^n/nx \, dx$.
- Draw graphs of $x^2+y^2=1$ and $x^3+y^3=1$.
- Draw graphs of $y=\sin x$ and $y=\sin^2 x$.
- Find the minimum value of x^2+6x+1.
- Prove that $\sqrt{2}$ or $\sqrt{3}$ is irrational.
- How does one find 2 to the power of $\sqrt{2}$?
- Prove that every fourth value of the Fibonacci series is a multiple of 3 and that every third value is even.
- Let $z=1+2i$. Show in an Argand diagram z, 3z, iz, /z/ and $\sqrt{z}$.
- Prove that in any function that maps from (0 to 1) to (0 to 1) there is at least one fixed point.

- Factorise the difference of two squares x^2-1
- Substitute into the above $(x+a)^2-b^2$

- Prove that $1+10^n$ cannot be a square number.
- Sketch the curve $y=\dfrac{2x^2+13x-8}{x^2-7}$
- Explain Product Rule from first principles.

- Find 0.999^9 to 3 decimal places.
- Prove that n^3-n is divisible by 6.
- Sketch $y=\dfrac{\cos x}{x+\pi/2}$
- Sketch $y=\dfrac{x}{\sin x}$ for $0 \le x \le 2\pi$.
- Which are your favourite topics in maths?
- How do you think science is portrayed in the media?
- What career are you interested in after your degree?

Students' comments

- 'The interview was very friendly and informal and when I was stuck with problems the interviewers were ready to prompt me.'

- 'The interview included a whole load of questions on differential equations. I also had to do a test for which calculators were not allowed (despite not being told this beforehand).'

- 'The interview was more a case of us working together on how to show integration as the opposite of differentiation. He didn't expect me to know how to do it, but he wanted to see how I could think my way through it and solve it with his help.'

- 'He said he was pleased to speak to someone who could have a conversation as opposed to just sitting down in silence. Reading *New Scientist* that morning proved to be a good idea!'

- 'You should practise sketching questions that have developmental parts. For example, sketch (1) $y=\sin x$, (2) $y=\sin^2 x$, (3) $y=\sin^2 x^2$.'

Media and communication studies

See sample questions under 'Journalism'.

Essential A levels A few courses specify English or media studies.
Useful A levels English, media studies, sociology and psychology.

Chance of being interviewed While many courses will make you an offer on the basis of your UCAS Apply, a significant minority of courses still interview.

What you need to know

- You need to be very clear about the sort of media course you are applying for. Some are more theoretical, others more practical. If yours is one of the more practical courses, do you know exactly what it will train you to do? Also, these courses by themselves will not normally guarantee you a job in the media. So, do your reasons for applying *correspond with* the content of the course?
- Many media courses will expect to see some sort of work experience or examples of taking initiative (for example, writing a sixth-form newsletter or contributing to a website).
- Try to think of examples (with evidence) of occasions when you have worked in a team. This is very important in media industries.
- Some courses may set you an extra test or assignment at the interview, usually to check your writing skills and spelling.

- Skillset is the Sector Skills Council for creative media covering: TV, film, radio, publishing, interactive media, computer games, photo imaging and facilities www.skillset.org.

Sample interview questions

- Define the word 'media'.
- Have you done any research into the media?
- Do you have any interests or hobbies that would be of benefit to a course in journalism?
- What are you hoping to do in the future?
- There are more people on media courses than there are jobs at the BBC. Why do you think you are going to get into this industry?
- How do you think your sociology A level will help you with this course?

- What impact do you think digital technology is having on the broadcasting industries?
- What is your favourite TV programme and why?
- Should the government renew the BBC's charter?
- How important is the *Today* programme on Radio 4?
- What is the difference between online and offline editing?
- What newspapers do you read? Talk about an article you read yesterday.

- Who is your favourite broadcast journalist?
- Have you recorded yourself speaking? In what way do you think your broadcast voice can be improved?
- Presuming that you have read a newspaper on the way to the interview, what story interested you most and why?
- Think of somebody who has a dreadful public image. How could we improve their reputation?
- Explain the formula for 'mission documentaries'.

Students' comments

- 'The interview day for my course in broadcast journalism involved a current affairs test and a group interview. The current affairs test was quite simple, but you do have to be well informed about recent news stories and past and present media magnates. I made a silly mistake from not being aware of the names of certain important media people! However, I think much of the selection process was based on how you presented yourself in the group interview. You have to be yourself and be clear.'

- 'I was expecting to be asked about my work experience. Most of the interview consisted of questions relating to media issues I had covered in sociology A level.'

Medicine

See also Chapter 5: "Applying for medicine'.

Essential A levels If you take chemistry, biology and one of maths or physics you will keep all the medical schools open to you. If you take chemistry and biology you will keep open the vast majority of them. If you do chemistry and one of maths or physics your range of choices will be much more limited.

Useful A/AS levels Critical thinking (this will help with section 3 of the BMAT test, however please make sure that critical thinking is done as a fifth AS Level).

Chance of being interviewed Expect to be interviewed by all of your choices.

What you need to know

- Most questions in an interview will relate to the content of your personal statement.
- You will be expected to explain fully why you want be become a doctor and provide evidence to back up your claims. What evidence do you have that proves you are genuinely interested in scientific issues and the welfare of others?
- If you have done some work experience in the fields of medicine or health, you will need to be able to explain what you learnt from this time.
- Know who the current Secretary of State for Health is and have some idea about how the National Health Service is funded. It is a good idea to be aware of some current issues or difficulties facing doctors. Is there one that you could talk about in more depth?
- You will probably be asked what qualities you think make a good doctor. Try to think of examples.
- Prepare yourself for any additional aptitude tests. See www.bmat.org.uk, www.ukcat.ac.uk.
- Some universities, for example King's College London and Southampton, are seeking to widen access to their medicine courses. Please see entry criteria in the prospectuses. These arrangements are for students who are facing significant barriers to achieving the grades normally required for medicine.
- For information on medical schools visit www.chms.ac.uk. Also visit the website of the British Medical Association – www.bma.org.uk.

Sample interview questions

- Why do you want to study medicine? How did you come to your decision?
- Has the fact that both your parents are doctors influenced your decision to apply for medicine?
- When did you first decide you wanted to become a doctor?
- What types of career do you think medicine offers?
- What are the disadvantages of medicine as a career?
- After qualifying as a doctor, how do you go on to become a consultant?
- Do you know what an elective is?
- What is a physician?

- Why medicine? Why not nursing?
- How important is research? Why?
- Who sets the curriculum for post-medical training?

- What qualities do you think a doctor should have?
- What qualities do *you* have that would contribute to this medical school?
- What steps have you taken to ensure that you will be suited to a medical career?
- How would you deal with the hard work and commitment needed on a medical course? Are you prepared for six years of study?
- Do you think medicine is stressful? How do you deal with stress and pressures?
- What do you think your life will be like as a doctor? What are your worries about being a doctor?
- How is general practice different from hospital medicine?

- What sort of person are you (for example, extrovert or introvert)? What are your good and bad points?
- What makes you angry or upset?
- Tell us about a problem and how you solved it.
- What makes you happy? What makes you sad?
- Do you consider yourself to be a perfectionist?
- Which do you prefer: conceptual stuff or nitty-gritty things?
- Are you more of a scientist or someone who likes working with people?
- What would you do it someone you were working with was not pulling their weight in your team?

- What would you do if your patient disagreed with your advice?
- Is there any type of person that you think you would not be able to handle?
- How would you feel treating a child with a terminal illness?
- How would you deal with death?
- Is it ethical to treat a patient who smokes/drinks/takes drugs?
- Are you a stranger to seeing people in pain?
- How would you cope with your first fatal mistake?
- Can you lead a group, or be part of a group led by someone else?
- What experience do you have of working in teams? Do you prefer working in a team or individually?
- Do you think medicine is a glamorous career?
- What problems do doctors face today?
- Is psychiatry something you would go into?
- How have people's attitudes towards doctors changed in the last fifteen years?
- Do you have a pessimistic or optimistic view of health care in this country?
- What do you think makes a good friend?

- Tell us about your work experience. What did you learn from it? Was it a daunting experience?
- What did your work experience show you about medicine?
- What was the highlight of your work experience?

- Tell us about your work shadowing. Have you watched how doctors work?
- Have you had any experience of a medical life? Have you visited hospitals or spoken to any doctors?
- Tell us about your voluntary work.
- Have you done any previous research?
- Describe a particular patient you saw on work experience.

- Have you read an article about health or medicine lately that has interested you? Tell us about it.
- Were there any ethical issues in the news recently?
- What literature do you think is the best for keeping you informed about medicine?
- What have you found interesting about medicine or medical ethics recently?
- What medical breakthroughs have taken place in the last 100 years?
- Name and discuss advances in medicine that have happened in the last five years.
- What medical advances do you think will happen in the next ten years?
- How do you think chemistry, biology or maths has influenced medicine in the last twenty years?
- What is the future of transplants?
- What is a retrovirus? How do retroviruses work?
- Why can we not (in practical terms) do the same with humans as we did with Dolly the cloned sheep?
- Do you know how genetic engineering works?
- What ethical problems can you see arising from genetic selection against disease?
- What do you think about the present state of the NHS. What do you think will happen to it in the near future? What do think about privatizing the NHS?
- If you could solve one problem in the NHS, with unlimited resources, what would it be?
- If you were head of the NHS what would you spend the money on?
- How do you think a surgeon decides who deserves any operation
- How should the NHS cope with an ever increasing ageing population?
- How can you justify spending £600,000 treating an overweight, drinking, smoking, middle-aged man instead of improving the health of seventy children?
- Do you feel more money needs to be spent on community medicine, i.e. prevention rather than cure?
- If a doctor has AIDS should he/she practise medicine?
- Does alternative medicine have a place in hospitals?
- Do you think people can 'think themselves better'? If so, what is the mechanism for this?

- What would you do if the Jehovah's Witness family of a patient refused a blood transfusion?
- On what criteria would you base decisions about who to treat and who to turn away?
- Who has the final say in a patient's treatment – the doctor, the patient or relatives?
- Should we cure people with cancer? Aren't they going to die anyway?
- If a child came to you with an injury, with the parents saying she fell, how would you check there was no problem of abuse at home?

- Do you agree with testing cosmetics on animals?
- Is medicine an art?

- What is your favourite topic in biology?
- What is the function of the skull? Why do new-born babies not have their skull cages fully fused?
- How do people turn their heads in all directions?
- How does blood get from your toes to your heart? What about at the venae cavae?
- Describe the structure of the heart.
- How does oxygen get from the air to your toes?
- Tell us about haemoglobin and the transportation of oxygen. What effect does high altitude have?
- Describe how air is inhaled and exhaled by mammals.
- What makes the body reject donated organs?
- Describe a neurone. How does an impulse travel down one?
- Why is an old person's long-term memory better than their short-term memory?
- Into what groups can amino acids be divided?
- How would a ketone react with an amine?
- You realise that a patient has been given a double dose of a drug by a doctor. What do you do?
- Why problem-based learning?
- What things have you done that show team work?
- What medical issues have you read about in the news lately?

Students' comments

- 'They basically wanted to know about me rather than my academic ability, despite this being an important factor. Also, it's useful to know about current events in relation to health and medicine, from articles and news reports.'

- 'If I didn't know something they gave clues to the answer. They seemed to want to know how I would think about finding the answer, rather than simply knowing it.'

- 'Be prepared for the usual questions: why medicine? why this medical school?'

- 'They seemed concerned about whether you were a normal person, able to cope with work as well as having hobbies, interests, etc.'

- 'They are very interested in anything you've done in or around medicine, such as work shadowing.'

- 'They were keen on probing about topical issues. In fact, much of the interview was spent trying to find out what I knew about the political side of medicine.'

Microbiology

See sample interview questions under: 'Biology'

Music

Essential A levels For most courses, music A level plus Grade VII or VIII.

Chance of being interviewed You should presume that you will be interviewed for all your choices and at interview you could be tested on one or many of the following areas (look at the prospectuses for the individual entry requirements for each course).

Performance	Aural
Keyboard	Harmony and counterpoint
Sight-singing	Extracts for analysis or 'naming of composer and period'

What you need to know

- Make sure that you are clear about the type of course you are applying for and why you want to do it. While there are still a large number of traditional courses, there has been a growth in popular and commercial music courses. Even among traditional courses, some put more emphasis on musicology while others emphasize performance.
- If you are very interested in performance, make sure that you can explain why you do not want to go to a *conservatoire*.
- You should expect questions to be based on the interests you have expressed in your personal statement. If you have mentioned a composer, expect questions on his or her use of instruments, harmony, counterpoint, time signatures and other compositional techniques, as well as historical setting, influences and so on.
- You need to have a wide grounding in music history – do not just rely on what you have studied for your music A level. As well as your areas of particular interest, you must have an overview of the Renaissance (1400-1600), baroque (1600-1750), classical (1750-1800), romantic (1800-1900) and modern (1900 onwards) periods.
- Visit the Incorporated Society of Musicians (www.ism.org) and the British Phonographic Industry (www.bpi.co.uk).
- Creative & Cultural Skills is the Sector Skills Council for advertising, crafts, cultural heritage, design, music, performing, literary and visual arts. www.ccskills.org.uk.
- Conservatoire Admissions Scheme: www.cukas.ac.uk.

Sample interview questions

- Do you enjoy performing?
- What sort of music do you like?
- Do you enjoy all types of music?
- What was the last concert you went to?

- Is there a performer you particularly admire?
- Have you written any original compositions? Describe them for us.
- Who has influenced your own compositions?
- What impact do you think digital technology is having on music?
- What is the role of live performance?
- How can you make a living in music?
- Do you think sequencing software is taking the skill out of music?

- Do you think Bach is an important composer?
- What do you learn from harmonizing in the style of Bach?
- What do you know about madrigals?
- Explain Haydn's influence on chamber music.
- How did Beethoven help develop the symphony?
- In the romantic period, what political and social changes affected composers?
- In what way did Debussy challenge the musical language of his time?
- What influenced Stravinsky?
- Why were patrons important?

Students' comments

- 'The most important part is your performance. I was asked to perform some Grade VIII flute music and I was also required to do some sight-reading and aural tests.'

- 'It was much simpler than I had been prepared for with my mock interview. The actual performance of the candidate is the top priority with most musicians, rather than any knowledge of musical history.'

NB These comments would not hold true for certain courses, for example at Oxford or Cambridge.

Natural sciences

See sample questions under 'Biology', 'Chemistry', 'Maths', 'Physics'.

Essential A levels Normally three out of biology, chemistry, maths and physics.

What you need to know

- While this course is well known as a Cambridge course, similar courses exist at a number of other universities as well.
- The course can really suit talented scientists who are not yet sure which direction they would like to take. It can also suit those who know what they would like to specialize in the future, but who want to cover more general science areas first.

Sample interview questions

- Draw a graph of a solid being heated.
- Why is it worse to be scalded by gas at 100°C than water at 100°C?
- Explain Newton's second law of motion, defining the terms you use.
- Describe and explain what is happening to a ruler balanced on one end when it falls on: a) smooth surfaces; b) rough surfaces. Why does the base slip?
- How would a body behave if it was removed from the plane of an ellipse of a solar system?
- Why do high tides occur twice in twenty-four hours?
- Why does an egg spin when it is hard boiled?
- How can waves travel through a vacuum?
- How does light behave as both a wave and a particle?
- Describe your last chemistry practical.
- What is the importance of photochemical reactions? How do they occur and how do they lead to the photoelectric effect?
- If you are religious, do you have a problem with Darwin's theory of evolution? What other theories of evolution are there?

- Talk about DNA and describe protein synthesis.
- What is the human genome project and why is it useful?
- Compare aerobic to anaerobic respiration.
- What type of rock is this [shown rock sample] and how can we date it?
- Why is it important to use fossils to date rocks?
- What problems are there with the environment?
- Talk about a scientific discovery that has revolutionized its field.

- Work out which is biggest and smallest, without evaluating, the integrals (all between e and 1) of: $\ln x$, $\ln(x^2)$, $(\ln x)^2$.

- What aspects of science are you interested in and why?
- Describe an article you have read recently in the *New Scientist* and discuss it.
- What is the last book you read?
- How aware should the public be about scientific developments?
- If I gave you a substance, what tests would you do to tell me what it was?
- The speed of computers doubles every one and a half years. Could you write an equation for this?
- Why does a bar magnet fall slower through a metal tube than a wooden one?
- Prove that in a game of pool, after a white ball collides with a red ball that is at rest, the velocities of the 2 balls are very nearly perpendicular.
- Is it possible to see an object through adjacent faces of a glass cube? (the refractive index of a glass is 1.5).
- A bouncy ball is dropped h metres from rest into a rigid wooden board inclined at 45° to the horizontal. Assuming no energy is lost in the collision, prove that the ball rebounds horizontally and find the distance it first bounces to the point it next bounces.

- How would you increase the efficiency of a bar heater with a fixed voltage across it?
- How does a mass spectrometer work?
- How does infrared stroboscopy work?

- Without integrating, rank in order of size: $\ln x\,dx$; $\ln x^2\,x$; $(\ln x)^2\,dx$.
- What is the difference in bonding that results in the difference in the nature of liquids (especially water), solids and gases?

- Describe what you can see (a monkey's brain in a jar).
- Compare the brain of a mouse with that of a human.
- Plan an experiment to show that a mouse does not have colour vision.
- Why do you think that human brain has so many folds in the cortex?
- How is a rat less complex than a human?
- Why would a rat not need colour vision?
- What interests you about genetics?
- Tell me about 'The Selfish Gene'.
- Describe what you can see (a tube of dirt, debris and seeds). How would you test for any living organism in this tube?
- What does this look like to you (shown a video clip of a small, moving insect). What do you think it is doing?

Students' comments

- 'I was asked academic questions on chemistry (addition polymerization, esterification), physics (metal stresses, simple harmonic motion) and maths (integration, polar coordinates). The interviewers deliberately chose topics that I said I hadn't covered in my A level studies. They are more interested in how you think and respond to new situations, than in how much you know. All you can do as preparation is brush up on you A level work to act as a foundation for the unfamiliar situations you will be presented with.'

- 'Whenever I told them that I hadn't yet covered certain topics at school they said, "Good, let's talk about it."'

- 'The interview opened with a question about what interested me in the subject and I mentioned an article I had read. He then asked me questions about this for nearly the whole interview. If I had realized, I would have mentioned a topic that I really knew about, rather than something I found fascinating but didn't know much about.'

- 'I was given thirty minutes to look over some unseen reading before the first interview. I then had to the sit a Thinking Skills Assessment (TSA) which was much harder than the practise provided online. I would recommend taking critical thinking A level."

Nursing and midwifery

See sample interview questions under: 'Professions allied to medicine'

Nutrition

See sample interview questions under: 'Professions allied to medicine' (dietetics) and 'Biology'

Occupational therapy

See sample interview questions under: 'Professions allied to medicine'

Optometry (ophthalmic optics)

Essential A levels Two from biology, chemistry, maths or physics (some courses prefer biology as one of the choices).

Chance of being interviewed You should expect some interviews.

What you need to know

- You will need to explain fully why you want be become an optometrist and provide evidence to back up your claims.
- If you have done some work experience in optometry, you will be asked to explain what you learnt from this time.
- It is a good idea to be aware of some current issues or difficulties facing optometrists Is there one that you could talk about in more depth?
- Think about what qualities you would need to be a good optometrist. Try to think of examples.
- Visit www.college-optometrists.org.

Sample interview questions

- Why do you want to study optometry?
- Where did your interest in optometry come from?
- What did you learn from work shadowing?
- When you were on your work experience, what eye defects did the optometrist have to deal with?

Students' comments

- 'I wasn't really asked anything about optometry. The interviewer seemed more interested in the personal section of my UCAS Apply.'

- 'The first question she asked was, "Why optometry?" You must be clear on this.'

Pharmacology

See sample interview questions under: 'Biology', 'Chemistry' and 'Pharmacy'

What you need to know

- Cogent is the Sector Skills Council for the chemicals and pharmaceuticals, oil and gas, petroleum and polymer industries. Visit www.cogent-ssc.org.

Pharmacy

Essential A levels Taking chemistry and two from biology, maths and physics will keep the vast majority of courses open to you. Some courses specify chemistry, biology and maths. Taking chemistry and biology keeps most courses open.

Chance of being interviewed You should expect to be interviewed by most of your choices.

What you need to know

- You will be asked to explain fully why you want be become a pharmacist and provide evidence to back up your claims.
- If you have done some work experience in pharmacy, you will need to be able to explain what you learnt from this time.
- It is a good idea to be aware of some current issues or difficulties facing pharmacists. Is there one that you could talk about in more depth?
- Try to identify anything that you have studied so far that relates to pharmacy. Be prepared to expand on this.
- Think about what qualities you need to be a good pharmacist. Try to think of examples.
- Visit the website of the Royal Pharmaceutical Society of Great Britain – www.rpsgb.org.uk.

Sample interview questions

- Why do you want to study pharmacy? Why not medicine?
- Have you had any practical experience of working in pharmacy?
- What do you think medical pharmacy involves?
- What other areas of pharmacy are there (for example, in industry)? What do you think they involve?
- What do you think is the role of the pharmacist?
- How did you find out about pharmacy? Have you done any research into careers in pharmacy?
- What career do you want to go into?

- Talk about a topic you are currently learning in biology or chemistry.
- How do you make a one-molar solution of sodium chloride?
- What does the liver do?
- What is an ECG (electrocardiogram)?
- What is the difference between a drug and a medicine?

Philosophy

Essential A levels None.
Useful A levels Maths, classical civilization, philosophy and religious studies/theology.

Chance of being interviewed Most courses will make offers on the basis of the UCAS Apply, but a significant minority of courses do still interview.

What you need to know

- A good starting point is to read *Philosophy: The Basics* by Nigel Warburton. Then try Bertrand Russell's *Problems of Philosophy*.
- You may be asked to sit a test or write an essay at the interview.
- Visit www.royalinstitutephilosophy.org.

Sample interview questions

- Why do you want to study philosophy?
- Have you read any books about philosophy?
- What interests you most about philosophy?

- Which of these three sentences are the most similar? All bats are blind. All mothers have babies. All water is made up of hydrogen and oxygen.

- If most lawyers are rich and most rich people live in the countryside and most country people go fishing on Sundays, does it follow that most lawyers go fishing on Sundays?
- If you keep adding grains of sand, one at a time, when does it become a heap? If you take away grains of sand one at a time, when does it stop being a heap? Is this a valuable intellectual debate?
- If it takes two to make a fight, when there's an argument are both sides equally to blame?
- I have promised my class a surprise exam one week in an eight-week term. Which week can I give it in?

- Why do we seek supernatural explanations for the unusual (for example, a tossed coin showing heads 1000 times) but not for the usual (for example, bodies obeying the laws of gravity)?
- If cosmic beliefs are religious, are religious beliefs cosmic?
- Discuss this statement: 'It has not yet been proven that God doesn't exist.'
- Does God exist?
- Is time travel possible?

- If your body is scanned, then destroyed and a perfect copy of you body and mind is instantaneously created on Mars and you 'wake up' there remembering everything, are you the same person?
- Is there more to a person than body and mind?
- Is teleporting a type of transport?
- Different societies have different moral standards. Is morality therefore subjective?

- Why is a bag of diamonds more expensive than a glass of water? When might this change?
- What is the difference between Mill's principles of utilitarianism and the rights of an individual?
- Can a business act morally when its aim is to maximize profits?
- Is it the nature of man to be altruistic or to promote his own interests?
- When is it OK to break a law? Who says when a law is unjust?
- How does one balance the views of two different cultures, for example in the case of the fatwa against Salman Rushdie?

Students' comments

- 'He assumed I had no prior knowledge of philosophy unless I told him otherwise.'

- 'It was very relaxed and informal and the discussion took the format of giving different arguments for and against several philosophical topics ranging from politics to theology.'

- 'Before the interview I was given a paper with five statements and arguments. I had twenty minutes to pick two to discuss in the interview. For example: "I might be wrong about anything I know. Therefore I might be wrong about everything I know."'

- 'I had to do a written test, stating the differences between words in pairs and then incorporating them in sentences to convey their meanings. The pairs were: accident/mistake; short/succinct; deny/refute; contradict/disprove; uninterested/disinterested.'

- 'He started to bombard me with unanswerable philosophical questions: "Why are we here?"; "What is life if it isn't a dream?" I was thoroughly confused and found it absurd and a little unfair that he expected me to answer such questions with no philosophical background at all, as if I had already done the course. He also looked remarkably like Benny Hill, which didn't help matters much!'

Photography

What you need to know

- Visit the websites of the Association of Photographers (www.the-aop.org) and the British Institute of Professional Photography (www.bipp.com).
- Skillset is the Sector Skills Council for creative media covering: TV, film, radio, publishing, interactive media, computer games, photo imaging and facilities www.skillset.org.
- Look at the sample interview questions under: 'Art and design', 'Media and communication studies'.
- Go to exhibitions
- Build up a portfolio of you own works.

Sample interview questions

- Who are your favourite photographers?
- What is it that inspires you about photography?
- Who inspires you?
- Why do you want to study photography?

Physics

See sample questions under 'Natural sciences'.

Essential A levels Maths and physics.
Useful A levels Further maths and chemistry.

Chance of being interviewed Most courses will make offers on the basis of what is in UCAS Apply, but a significant minority of courses do still interview.

What you need to know

- Interview questions will tend to relate to what you have already studied at A level (including mechanics and pure maths), as well as subjects you have mentioned on your personal statement.
- Sometimes there may be a test at the interview. This could be written or the questions could be asked orally.
- Look at relevant questions under 'Natural Sciences'.
- Visit the website of the Institute of Physics – www.iop.org.

Sample interview questions

- What area of physics interests you most? Would you like to specialize in this area?
- Give an example of your problem solving abilities.
- What are the four basic forces in physics?

- If a centripetal force is acting inwards, why do you feel thrown outwards when travelling around a bend in a car?
- If an anchor is thrown out of a boat into a lake, will the water level of the lake rise or fall?
- Are the molecules in a solid stationary?
- If you displaced a molecule in a solid and then let go, would it go back to its original position?
- Why do light spectra radiate from the centre of the surface of a compact disc?
- What is the equation explaining a star's orbit in its galaxy?
- Explain why it is suggested that dark matter is what keeps stars in orbit at a constant relational velocity even as they are found further from the centre of a galaxy.
- Being in space is associated with weightlessness. What does weightlessness mean to you?
- Galileo timed light and heavy objects rolling down inclined planes. How do you think he timed the rolling?
- Would you expect all records to be broken were the Olympic Games to be held in a hall on the moon?
- A sheet of white paper is viewed through a piece of blue glass and the paper looks blue. Why?
- What do you know about the ways in which atoms are arranged in a solid. What happens when the atoms in a solid are heated?

- What is the relationship between the number of molecules of gas per unit volume and the number that hit area A, with velocity v in time t?
- Give me an equation relating energy and distance.
- Differentiate $v^2 e^{-av}$.
- Work out the equation for the power of a wind turbine and how wind speed affects it.
- Estimate the time taken for a jumbo jet to fly from London to Sydney.

For astrophysics:
- Tell us what you know about the origins and evolution of the universe.
- What is the Hubble constant?
- Does the earth turn clockwise or anticlockwise?

Students' comments

- 'I was also asked some maths questions about integration and something else to do with complex numbers that we hadn't covered at school yet.'

- 'Questions were asked on everything we have done for A level so far. The questions were occasionally badly worded making it difficult to understand what was wanted.'

- 'The interviewers were happy to give help if they saw you were in trouble and did not just leave you to baffle over the questions.'

Physiology

Essential A levels Chemistry and biology would keep most courses open.
Useful A levels Maths and physics.

Chance of being interviewed Most courses will make you an offer on the basis of what is in UCAS Apply but a significant minority of courses do still interview.

What you need to know

- See sample interview questions under: 'Biology' and 'Medicine'

Sample interview questions

- Why did you apply specifically for physiology?
- Why not medicine?
- What are you looking to gain from the course and the university?
- What medical/biological stories have you read in the news recently?

- What do you think about animal testing?
- How would you argue against someone saying testing drugs on rats can have little or no benefit to a human because they are different creatures?
- Can pain in animals be justified? To what extent can pain be inflicted for the benefit of human research?
- How does a neurone act? How does it work?
- What is the importance of a myelin sheath? What would happen if it was removed?
- How can a DNA mutation occur?
- What is the shape of a synapse?
- Name some neurotransmitters.
- What neurodegenerative disorders do you know of? Tell me about one.
- Do you know what causes schizophrenia or multiple sclerosis?
- MS is caused by the degradation of the myelin sheath. Suggests causes for this.
- MS is genetically inherited. Why doesn't everyone with the MS gene contract MS?
- Why doesn't MS affect someone from birth if it is in their genes?
- What is the immune system?
- What environmental factors could affect whether or not someone gets MS?
- Why could viruses affect whether the person gets MS or not?
- What is the difference between a pump and a channel.
- Describe the reabsorption mechanism of the kidney?
- If two parents are homozygous recessive for albinism, how can they have a child you is not an albino?
- If neither parent is an albino, how can they have a child that is?
- What is the main disease in the UK that needs to be researched compared to that in the world as a whole?

Students' comments

'I was given 25 minutes to write an essay on 'Plumbers save more lives than doctors. Discuss.''

'I was asked a really complicated question on blood pressures, given different tubes and asked to draw many graphs!'

Physiotherapy

See sample interview questions under: 'Professions allied to medicine'

Podiatry

See sample interview questions under: 'Professions allied to medicine'

Politics

Essential A levels None.
Useful A levels Politics, economics, history, philosophy, sociology, law.

Chance of being interviewed Most courses will make you an offer on the basis of what is in UCAS Apply but a significant minority of courses do still interview.

What you need to know

- If you are not taking politics A level, you should still have done some reading around political philosophies, political history and the workings of government.
- You need to be aware of the political world around you, by following current affairs.
- Try to find out more about the politics of a country other than the UK.
- Questions at interview will tend to be based on your current studies and what you have put in your personal statement.
- Visit www.psa.ac.uk.

Sample interview questions

- Why are you interested in politics?
- What political ideology are you most attracted to?
- How active are you in politics and what are your views?
- Who would you vote for in a general election and why?
- Tell us what you think about the current political situation in Britain.

- Does your vote count?
- Is Britain a democracy? How could it be made more democratic?
- What are your views on electoral reform?
- What system of proportional representation should Britain introduce?
- What do you think about reform of the House of Lords?
- Does Britain need a bill of rights?
- Discuss the differences between the views and policies of the Labour, Conservative and Liberal Democrat Parties.
- What do you think about devolution in Scotland and Wales?
- Ken Livingstone was first elected mayor of London as an independent, not as a Labour candidate. What is the difference between a political party and an individual?
- What would you do if you were prime minister?
- Account for the enduring reputation of Margaret Thatcher.

- What do you think about Europe and the European Union?
- Does Britain have control of its monetary policy when it is part of the European Union?
- What do you think about the euro?

- If there is a more federal Europe, what control would Britain have over its own policy?
- Why is Britain uncompetitive?

- Do the media provide impartial reporting?
- Is there, or should there be, censorship of the media?
- Do the owners of newspapers determine their content?
- How aware do you think the general British public is about politics?

- What are the differences between the political systems of the United States and the United Kingdom?
- What do you know about American politics?
- How would you define a developing country?
- Why do you think some countries are developed and others underdeveloped?
- Why should we give aid to other countries?
- In what ways was the conflict in Northern Ireland similar to the current situation in the Middle East?
- What do you think about Zimbabwe?

- Define ideology.
- Is environmentalism an ideology?
- Tell us about Marxism.
- What is the main principle of liberalism?
- What is the difference between power and authority?
- Distinguish between: right and good; just and fair; nation and state.
- What role does economics play in politics?
- What should the role of the church be in politics?
- Comment on this statement: 'It is inevitable that there will be conflict between state and freedom.'
- Do you think we are freer with laws?

- What period of history are you most interested in? What have you learned from it?
- Could dictators such as Hitler arise in the present day?
- Map out the history of Russia, up to the present day, for someone who knows nothing at all about it.
- What are you reading?
- Name a book that has had an effect on your view of politics or economics.
- Comment on the way some European nation states have retained their monarchies. What have you read related to this?
- Do you perceive Barack Obama to be black, white, Kenyan, American?
- Why do you think the working class majorities did not rise up against the Liberals in the 1800s and redistribute wealth?

Students' comments

- 'The interviewer asked very general political questions, such as "Is Marxism dead?" and let me lead on to subjects I felt strong in.'

- 'They didn't ask any particularly interesting questions but they did persist on every point I made and forced me to really develop every answer.'

- 'The interview would have been a lot harder had I not done politics A level.'

- 'Before the interview we had to read a passage about the merits and demerits of the welfare state, and two tables of results from the French elections in 1958 and 1962. I had to answer questions on these in the interview, for example saying what the election results indicated. It was tricky stuff and I felt I kept getting things wrong.'

- 'It was very personal. I was asked who I would vote for in a general election, and who my parents vote for and why.'

Professions allied to medicine

Dietetics
Essential A levels Chemistry and biology.

Nursing and midwifery
Essential A levels Some courses ask for biology or another science.

Occupational therapy
Essential A levels Some courses ask for biology. Some will also consider psychology, physical education, sociology or another science.

Physiotherapy
Essential A levels Most courses will consider you with just biology. However, some ask for a second science from chemistry, maths or physics.

Podiatry
Essential A levels Courses normally require at least one science, and usually prefer biology. Some courses specify biology plus another science.

Radiography
Essential A levels Most courses ask for one science A level, a few ask for two.

Speech and language therapy
Essential A levels Some courses require a science such as biology, chemistry or physics (some specify biology). However, some will consider candidates with none of these.
Useful A levels A modern foreign language (French, German, Spanish, Italian), English language (and literature), psychology.

Chance of being interviewed You should expect to be interviewed and prepare for this.

What you need to know

- **Dietetics** The dietician's skill is to translate the science of nutrition into understandable and practical information about food and health. Contact the website of the British Dietetic Association (www.bda.uk.com).
- **Nursing and midwifery** These courses train you to become a hospital or community nurse, health visitor or midwife. Contact NHS Careers (www.nhscareers.nhs.uk), the Royal College of Nursing (www.rcn.org.uk) and the Royal College of Midwives (www.midwives.co.uk).
- **Occupational therapy** This can also be called rehabilitation therapy. It is concerned with helping people with physical and mental disorders to live a full life by overcoming as much as possible the effects of their disability. Contact the College of Occupational Therapy (www.cot.co.uk).
- **Physiotherapy** Physiotherapists use exercises and movement, electrotherapy, manipulation and massage to treat the injured, disabled, sick and convalescents of all ages for a large variety of conditions. Contact the Chartered Society of Physiotherapy (www.csp.org.uk).
- **Podiatry** The Society for Chiropodists and Podiatrists can be found at www.feetforlife.org.
- **Radiography** Diagnostic radiographers use X-rays, ultrasound and magnetic resonance imaging to produce images of the body. Therapeutic radiographers are involved in the treatment of cancer. Contact the Society of Radiographers (www.sor.org).
- **Speech therapy** Speech and language therapists assess and treat all kinds of voice, speech, language and swallowing problems. Contact the Royal College of Speech and Language Therapists (www.rcslt.org).
- For all the above career area www.nhscareers.nhs.uk.

- You will need to be able to explain fully why you want to enter your chosen career and provide evidence to back up your claims.
- If you have done some work experience that relates to this career, you will be expected to explain what you learnt from it.
- It is a good idea to be aware of some current issues or difficulties associated with this career. Is there one that you could talk about in more depth?
- Think about what qualities you would need for this career. Try to think of examples.

Sample interview questions

- What do you see as the role of a nurse?
- Why do you want to do nursing?
- Why do you particularly want to do children's nursing?
- What qualities do you have that would make you a good nurse?
- In what ways would you help a stroke victim?

- Why do you want to be a physiotherapist? How did you get involved in physiotherapy and how long have you been interested in it?
- What qualities do you think a physiotherapist needs. Do you have them?
- What does physiotherapy involve?
- What areas do physiotherapists work in?
- What steps did you take to find out more about physiotherapy before you applied?
- What did you learn from you work experience?
- Are your A levels relevant to physiotherapy?
- What do physics and maths have to do with physiotherapy?

- Why do you want to do speech therapy?
- What sparked your interest in such a specialized area?
- What qualities does a speech therapist need? Do you have them?
- Tell us about your work placement. What did you learn from it? Did it reaffirm your decision to do speech therapy?
- What have you learned from speech therapy clinics you have visited?
- Have your A levels taught you anything that would be relevant to speech therapy?
- Have you read any books about speech therapy?
- What do the terms 'linguistics', 'phonetics' and 'neurological impulses' mean to you?
- How does phonetics work?
- Do you think there are medical and teaching elements in a speech therapist's work?
- What are the problems with speech therapy?
- Why might parents not take their child to speech therapy sessions?
- Do you think deaf people should be encouraged to use sign language or learn verbal skills?
- Courses in this area have various names – speech therapy, speech science, speech pathology. Are there differences? What do you know about this particular course?

- Why do you want to do midwifery?
- When have you faced conflict and how did you deal with it?
- What is the role of a midwife?
- Have people been negative about you choosing midwifery?

- What are the differences between working as a dietician in a hospital and in the school meals service?
- What issues face dieticians?
- What topics have you studied for your chemistry A level that relate to nutrition?

- Why do you want to become an occupational therapist?
- On your work experience did you see the occupational therapists working with other professionals? How did they do this?
- What do you think occupational therapy involves?

- Which types of patient do podiatrists come into contact with?
- What did you learn from your time at a podiatry clinic?

- Which other professionals would use a radiography department?
- What is the difference between diagnostic and therapeutic radiography?

Students' comments

- 'We watched a video (about one-and-a-half minutes long) about a man who had suffered a stroke and the effect it had had on his speech. Then we had to discuss it in the interview.'

- 'We had to take part in a one-hour activity about delayed auditory feedback, which we had to answer questions on afterwards.'

- 'As part of my physiotherapy interview they asked to see my hands, to check for any problems.'

- 'My first physiotherapy interview included a physical examination, which was not a problem. However, while I was getting dressed I was being asked several questions at the same time so, between ripping my tights and putting my jumper on, my answers were slightly muffled!'

Psychology

Essential A levels A few courses ask for one of biology, chemistry, maths or physics.
Useful A levels Biology, maths, psychology and sociology.

Chance of being interviewed Only a small number of courses interview applicants.

What you need to know

- If you want to become a professional psychologist, make sure the course has been accredited by the British Psychological Society.
- Psychology degree courses do not involve helping people with their problems! You will be studying subjects such as personality types, defining and testing intelligence, perception, memory and developmental psychology.

- The main reasons for rejection are a lack of reading about psychology and not understanding what is involved in a psychology degree course.
- It is helpful to know the differences between the different branches of psychology: clinical psychology; educational psychology; occupational psychology; criminal and legal psychology.
- Visit the website of the British Psychological Society (www.bps.org.uk).

Sample interview questions

- Why do you want to study psychology?
- What aspects of psychology are you particularly interested in?
- Why do you want to do a BSc in experimental psychology rather than a BA in psychology?
- Why do you particularly want to do social psychology?
- What do you want to do after your psychology degree?

- What books have you read about psychology?
- What have you learnt about psychology through your other A level subjects?
- What do you think you will be studying in the first year of your psychology course?

- Do you know what a psychology experiment is? Have you ever carried one out?
- Design a psychology experiment concerning colour blindness.
- How could you devise an experiment to find out if animals see in black and white?
- What is perception?
- What is the benefit to psychologists of a person who has been blind all their life and then regains their sight?
- Do you think Milgram's obedience studies could be done again?

Student's comment

- 'There was no need to be nervous. You just have to know why you want to do your course and be confident.'

Quantity surveying

See sample interview questions under: 'Surveying' and 'Accountancy'.

Radiography

See 'Professions allied to medicine'

Religious studies and theology

Essential A levels None.
Useful A levels Religious studies/theology, philosophy, English literature, history.
Chance of being interviewed Most courses will make offers on the basis of what is in UCAS Apply, but a significant minority of courses still interview.

What you need to know

- There is no need to be religious to study many of these degrees. In fact, if you are very conservative in your beliefs you may not enjoy the majority of courses in this field.
- An attempt to gain some knowledge of a broad range of religions will be welcomed.
- Questions in interviews will generally be based on your current studies, information you have put in your personal statement and topical issues.
- Visit www.multifaithcentre.org.

Sample interview questions

- Why do you want to study theology?
- Why do you want to study divinity rather than religious studies?

- Do you believe in a God? How can you prove his existence?
- What is a miracle?
- What do you think about 'Pascal's wager'?
- What other religions interest you as well as Christianity? Why?
- Do we need religion to understand human existence?
- What do you think the influence of Socrates has been?
- What do you think is the importance of religious architecture?
- What are your views on genetic engineering?
- What do you think is the difference between theology and philosophy?

Student's comment

- 'I was given a pack on Genesis and then had to make a presentation on how relevant Genesis 1 and 2 were for a contemporary theology of creation.'

Social policy

See sample interview questions under: 'Politics', 'Sociology', 'History' and 'Economics'

Social work

Essential A levels None.
Useful A levels AGCE/Diploma health and social care, sociology, psychology, law.
You must have grade C or above in English and maths GCSE.

What you need to know

- You will need to show an understanding of social and community work at a basic level. Read *Introduction to Social Work* by Coulshed and Orm.
- You must have an understanding of, and an ability to define the meaning of, discrimination. What does it mean? How does it manifest itself? How can it be challenged?
- You will need to demonstrate a commitment to this career path through work experience (paid or voluntary).
- All candidates have to be police checked (but a criminal conviction will not automatically exclude you).
- Read *Anti-Discriminatory Practice* by Neil Thompson, published by Palgrave Macmillan.
- Visit www.gscc.org.uk and www.socialworkcareers.co.uk.

Sample interview questions

- What does a social worker do?
- Can you talk about some of the issues affecting social work in general?
- Think about your voluntary work or work experience. Can you think of two changes you would make that would have improved the service delivered?

- What qualities and skills do you think a social worker needs?
- What qualities and skills do you think you can bring to social work?
- Which of your qualities and skills would you like to develop or improve while you are on the course?

- What has been your experience of academic life to date?
- Can you talk about an idea or theory that you have studied that has influenced your views?

- Can you give an example of discrimination that you have experienced or observed? How was this dealt with?
- If you were faced with an unpleasant scenario (for example, having to interview an aggressive parent who has been mistreating their young child) how do you believe you would cope?
- What client group would you like to deal with on qualification? Why?
- Should disabled students go to mainstream schools?

Sociology

Essential A levels None.
Useful A levels History, politics, sociology, psychology, geography and media studies.
Chance of being interviewed Most courses will make offers based on the content of the UCAS Apply, though a minority of courses do still interview.

What you need to know

- If you are not taking sociology A level, you should do some introductory reading on the key themes of: social theory; social change; social identities and structures.
- Interview questions will tend to be based on your current studies and on issues you have raised in your personal statement.
- It is a good idea to keep abreast of current affairs and issues that interest you that affect society, past, present and future.
- Visit www.britsoc.co.uk.

Sample interview questions

- Why do you want to study sociology?
- What are you looking for from a course on sociology?
- State three social problems that exist in Britain and explain them.

- As a sociologist, how would you explain crime?
- Why do eighteen-year-olds commit crimes?
- Can schools play an important role in reducing criminal behaviour, particularly among eighteen-year-olds?
- Are single-parent families a symptom or a cause of instability in society?
- What is social policy?
- What newspapers do you read? What makes a good columnist?
- What books do you read?
- If you went to India to do marital relationships research and found that the norm was to marry for practicality, not romance, but then found that the major Bollywood hit at the time was based on romantic relationships what would you make of it?

Students' comments

- 'Be topical. Have a listen to the news or read the paper on the day of the interview.'

- 'I mentioned that I was interested in crime and deviance, which I had studied at AS level. This led to a long discussion. If you're going to bring something up, read up on it first.'

Speech therapy

See 'Professions Allied to Medicine'

Sport and physical education

Essential A levels Many courses want to see one of biology, chemistry, maths, or physics.
Useful A levels Physical education, psychology.

Chance of being interviewed Most courses will make offers on the basis of the UCAS Apply but a significant minority of courses do still interview.

What you need to know

- You need to be clear about the type of course you are applying for. Sports courses tend to cover physiology, psychology, sports performance, coaching and the business and administration of sport. A leisure management course will be more like a business studies course, a sports journalism course is a journalism course, a sports therapy course is closer to a physiotherapy course.
- Interviewers will be very interested in your sporting history to date. Reread your personal statement to make sure you got this across. However, being a talented sportsperson is not enough in itself to get you on to a course.
- Visit the websites of Sport England (www.sportengland.org) and the Central Council of Physical Recreation (www.ccpr.org.uk).
- SkillsActive is the Sector Skills Council for the active leisure and learning industry embracing sport and fitness, outdoors and adventure, playwork, camping and caravanning. www.skillsactive.com.

Sample interview questions

- How can we get more children involved in sport?
- Why do you want to do a degree in sports science?
- What is your favourite sport and why?
- Why do you think football is much more popular than hockey in the UK?
- How do you think you could improve your sporting performance?
- Why do you want to train as a PE teacher after this degree?
- Do you agree that athletes using banned substances should not be allowed to compete?
- If you are so interested in physiology, why haven't you applied for a physiotherapy degree?
- What is the best sort of diet for your sport? Why?
- Are you considering a career related to sport?
- Why do you think the armed forces encourage so much sporting activity?

- What do you think is the best way to coach children in your sport?

Statistics

See sample interview questions under: 'Maths'

Surveying

Essential A levels None.
Useful A levels For some types of surveying (for example, building surveying) maths and physics could be helpful. For estate management (general practice surveying) most A level combinations will be considered.

Chance of being interviewed Most courses will make offers on the basis of the UCAS Apply, however a significant minority of courses do still interview.

What you need to know

- Surveying is the measurement, management, development and valuation of anything and everything – whether it is natural or man-made.
- There are different types of surveying. The main ones are: general practice surveying (valuation, estate agency, auctioneering and property development); quantity surveying (building accountants); building surveying; land surveying; mineral surveying.
- For more information, contact the Royal Institute of Chartered Surveyors (www.rics.org.uk).
- Interviewers will be concerned with why you want to enter this career field and what you have done to find out about it, for example through work experience.

Sample interview questions

- Why do you want to do quantity surveying?
- Do you know what quantity surveying is?
- What do you know about quantity surveying? How did you find out about it?

- Why are you interested in a career in property?
- Do you know the difference between retail and commercial property?
- What is 'buy to let'?

- When you did your work experience, what kind of business was the company you went to involved in?

- What experience do you have of dealing with customers?
- You have done arts A levels. How will you cope with some of the technical parts of the course?
- What will you do with your degree?

Tourism

What you need to know

- Look at the sample interview questions under 'Business studies'. Most of these courses are a business degree with a travel and tourism slant.
- Think about any positive or negative experiences you have had whenever you have left your normal environment.
- Try to think of any evidence that you can provide about your personal qualities (for example, communication skills).
- Visit www.tournet.org and www.uksp.co.uk.

Town and country planning

What you need to know

- You will need to explain fully why you want to enter this career and provide evidence to back up your claims.
- If you have done some work experience that relates to this career, you will be expected to explain what you learnt from this time.
- It is a good idea to be aware of some current issues or difficulties associated with this career. Is there one that you could talk about in more depth? Perhaps you could visit a new town in the UK.
- Think about the qualities you would need for this career. Try to think of examples.
- Look at the sample interview questions under 'Geography' ,'Architecture' and 'Surveying'.
- Visit www.rtpi.org.uk.

Veterinary science

Essential A levels You need to take chemistry and biology, plus either maths or physics, in order to keep all six courses open to you.

Chance of being interviewed Expect to be interviewed by all of your choices.

What you need to know

- You will need to explain fully why you want to become a vet and provide evidence to back up your claims.
- It is important to have done some relevant work experience and be able to explain what you learnt from it. To play safe, you should have done two weeks in a veterinary practice, two weeks with large domestic animals or livestock and two weeks with others animals (kennels, stables, zoo, etc.).
- It is a good idea to be aware of some current issues or difficulties facing vets. Is there one that you could talk about in more depth?
- Some Vet Schools will want you to take the BMAT www.bmat.org.uk.
- Think about what qualities you would need to be a vet. Try to think of examples.
- Visit the website of the Royal College of Veterinary Surgeons (www.rcvs.org.uk).

Sample interview questions

- Why do you want to read veterinary science?
- Which of the sciences do you prefer? Why?
- Which aspect of biology do you enjoy most?
- What work experience have you had that is relevant to veterinary science?

- What dilemmas do vets face in their profession?
- Talk about the quarantine laws with respect to rabies.
- How do vaccinations work?
- With respect to mammals, are herbivores on the whole larger than carnivores? Why are they larger?
- Horses and cattle have similar digestive systems? What disease do they have in common?
- What do you think about current farming methods? How would you change them?
- What are your views on animal experimentation?
- If you felt a pig farmer was being cruel to his livestock, what would you do?
- Are you a vegetarian?
- Could there be an NHS for animals?
- Could the government have handled the foot and mouth crisis differently?

- How are physics and maths applied to veterinary science?
- Describe an experiment you have carried out in one of your science subjects. Explain what happened and why.

- Talk about the cell membrane. Give an example of a substance that protein molecules allow into the cell.
- Where does respiration occur in cells? Explain the theory behind the presence of mitochondria in cells.
- Talk about the differences between gases, liquids and solids, with particular reference to water.
- Would you rather be a caged rabbit or a wild rabbit?

Zoology

See sample interview questions under: 'Biology' and 'Veterinary science'

Index of university subjects